ALONE THROUGH
THE ROARING FORTIES

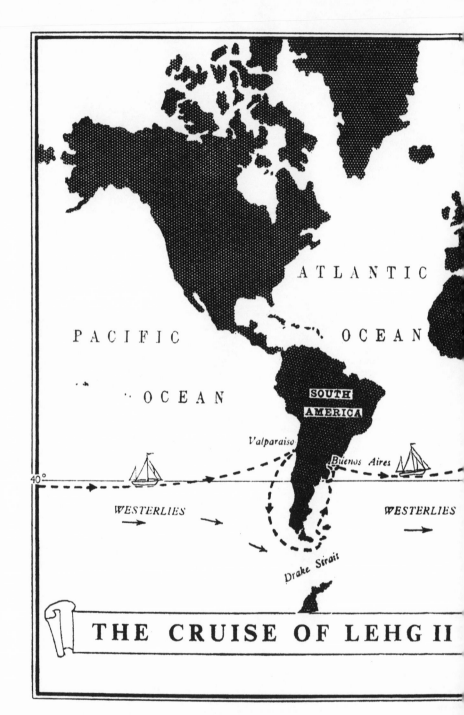

PACIFIC

OCEAN

ATLANTIC

OCEAN

SOUTH
AMERICA

Valparaiso

Buenos Aires

40°

WESTERLIES

WESTERLIES

Drake Strait

THE CRUISE OF LEHG II

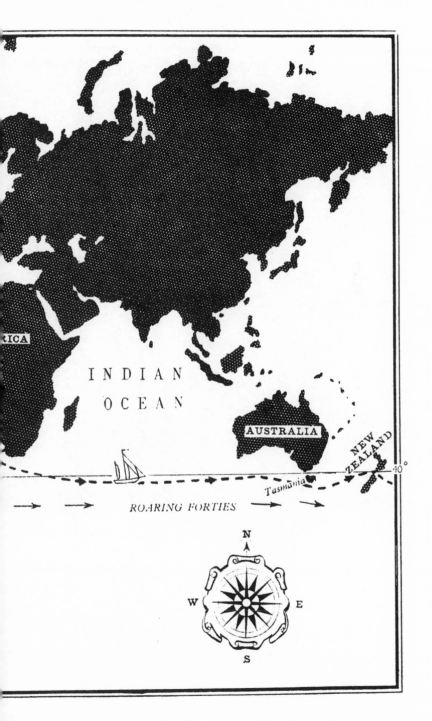

Vito Dumas in oilskins. Taken aboard *Lehg II* at Cape Town.

ALONE THROUGH THE ROARING FORTIES

The voyage of *Lehg II* round the world

by Vito Dumas

Translated by Captain Raymond Johnes

Introduction by Jonathan Raban

INTERNATIONAL MARINE / McGRAW-HILL

Camden, Maine • New York • Chicago • San Francisco • Lisbon •
London • Madrid • Mexico City • Milan • New Delhi • San Juan • Seoul •
Singapore • Sydney • Toronto

Other titles in
The Sailor's Classics series:

40,000 Miles in a Canoe and Sea Queen, *John C. Voss*

Gipsy Moth Circles the World, *Francis Chichester*

Once Is Enough, *Miles Smeeton*

The Saga of Cimba, *Richard Maury*

The Strange Last Voyage of Donald Crowhurst, *Tomalin and Hall*

International Marine

A Division of The McGraw·Hill Companies

10 9 8 7 6 5 4 3 2 1
Copyright © 1960 Adlard Coles Ltd.
Introduction copyright © 2001 Jonathan Raban

Library of Congress Cataloging-in-Publication Data
Dumas, Vito.
    Alone through the roaring forties : the voyage of Lehg II round the world / by Vito Dumas ; translated by Captain Raymond Johnes ; introduction by Jonathan Raban
            p.   cm.
    ISBN 0-07-137611-9 (hardcover : alk. paper)
        1. Dumas, Vito—Journeys. 2. Lehg II (Ketch) 3. Voyages around the world.   I. Title.
    G440.D86 D86 2001
    910.4′1—dc21   2001002833

This book is printed on 55# Sebago by R.R. Donnelley, Crawfordsville, IN.
Design by Dennis Anderson
Page layout by Eugenie Delaney
Production management by Janet Robbins

CONTENTS

Introduction by Jonathan Raban   XIII

Translator's Foreword   XXV

Introduction   XXX

ONE
The Search for a Mate   1

TWO
My Faith in *Lehg II*   7

THREE
Good Luck   10

FOUR
The 27th of June   12

FIVE
The Great Day   18

SIX
The Arm and the Sea   25

SEVEN
Prevailing Storms   29

EIGHT
Human Voices at Last   38

NINE
Start Again   46

TEN
. . . And Carry On   49

ELEVEN
Buenas Tardes, Señor   52

TWELVE
Washing Up   54

THIRTEEN
The Worst of All   60

FOURTEEN
Legends of the Sea   62

FIFTEEN
My Friend the Pigeon   74

SIXTEEN
Slow Death   81

SEVENTEEN
"Upon a Painted Ocean"   84

EIGHTEEN
The Visitor Arrives   87

NINETEEN
No Can Chew   94

TWENTY
City of the Winds   103

TWENTY-ONE
The Dash for America   107

TWENTY-TWO
Whose Little Slipper?   116

TWENTY-THREE
The Last Slice   119

TWENTY-FOUR
A Secret Is Revealed   124

TWENTY-FIVE
Dead Man's Road   127

TWENTY-SIX
In Search of the Atlantic   136

TWENTY-SEVEN
Done It!   141

TWENTY-EIGHT
Four Minutes Slow   145

TWENTY-NINE
Recessional   148

THIRTY
A Letter   149

THIRTY-ONE
The Rescue   151

THIRTY-TWO
The Yacht for the Job   153

THIRTY-THREE
We're Here   158

APPENDIX I
Principal Passages of Vito Dumas   163

APPENDIX II
Commentary on the Conception and Design of
Lehg II by Manuel M. Campos, Naval Architect   165

APPENDIX III
Opinion of Vito Dumas on *Lehg II*   169

LIST OF ILLUSTRATIONS

Vito Dumas in oilskins. Taken aboard *Lehg II* at Cape Town   iv

The Author on horse-back on his country estate near
   Buenos Aires   xxxi

Lehg II being painted and re-fitted at the Argentine
   Yacht Club before departure   xxxii

Lehg II is given a good send-off at Cape Town   55

Lehg II starting from Cape Town Harbour at the beginning
   of her passage through the Indian Ocean   56

Lehg II sailing near Buceo Harbour at the end of the voyage   161

An enthusiastic crowd waiting for Vito Dumas to go
   ashore at Buenos Aires harbour at the end of his voyage
   round the world   162

LIST OF DIAGRAMS

Map of route taken by Vito Dumas in his single-handed
   voyage round the world   xxiv

Lehg II turns over   9

Map showing route taken by *Lehg II* from Valparaiso to
   Mar Del Plata, via Cape Horn   130

Lehg II. Designed by Manuel M. Campos   167

*The sketches have been drawn by Mr. C. Kingston from originals
supplied by the Author*

INTRODUCTION TO THE SAILOR'S CLASSICS EDITION

Jonathan Raban

IF THE ACCOUNTS of long-distance single-handed voyaging have a single dominant theme, it is that the character of the sailor is transformed—and redeemed—by the sea. When Joshua Slocum set off to sail around the world in *Spray*, he was on the run from an unbearable marriage and an unsavory reputation as a bullying "bucko" captain in the merchant marine. On land, Slocum was in the habit of getting himself into big trouble (he appeared in court three times, on charges of wrongful imprisonment, murder, and indecency); at sea, alone, he found the peace of mind that eluded him ashore, and the wry, reflective sweetness of tone that makes *Sailing Alone around the World* an uncontested masterpiece of small-boat literature.

A similar kind of sea change is at work in Vito Dumas's *Alone through the Roaring Forties*—the most endearingly humble and intimate narrative of one of the greatest voyages ever made by a solo sailor. Dumas's three-stop circumnavigation of the world, at latitudes infamous for their extended gales and appallingly high seas, was accomplished in a cruising ketch, less than 32 feet in length, without self-steering gear, in the middle of a major war. It's hard to imagine a more punishing, or more unrepeatable, feat of seamanship and navigation.

The marvelous thing about this book is that Dumas makes so little of his own heroic fortitude. Instead the reader meets not a driven loner, but a man who is sociable to a fault, equally addicted to the conversation of cultivated women and the roistering life of dockside bars. Dumas emerges from his writing as the least obsessive, least hard-bitten of all the great singlehanders. Here is someone whose last appointment on shore is with his manicurist, and who breaks down into tears when he sails away from his family and friends.

The brutal severity of the voyage would have justified a book that was little more than a record of distances, sail changes, sun sights, and marine shenanigans. But Dumas chose to see his circumnavigation as a test of his ordinary humanity. There are hurricane-force winds here, and horrendous waves, but they take second place to Dumas's domestic life—kneeling by his bunk each night to say his prayers, making fresh underwear out of a sack lined with newspaper, communing with a fly—and it is his reverence for the small things that gives *Alone through the Roaring Forties* its distinction as a classic. This most harrowing of voyages is presented by its author as a story of Everyman on a modest sea pilgrimage.

DUMAS WAS AN ARTIST before he was a sailor. His translator, Raymond Johnes, compares him with "the cosmic artists of the Renaissance," which is laying it on a little thick, but after leaving school early to help out with the family finances (his father, a tailor, ran an ailing one-man business in a Buenos Aires back street), Dumas received some formal art school training. He sold seascapes (mostly to a generous bartender), and made appearances as a singer on Argentine radio. Unusually, his ambition to make his mark on the world as an artist went hand in hand with a passion to excel at sport.

As a young man, he supported himself by giving swimming lessons, and it was as a record-breaking swimmer that he first tried to gain the fame he craved. He made half a dozen attempts to swim the 40-kilometer-wide River Plate from Colonia in Uruguay to Punta Lara in Argentina, but he was beaten by bad weather every time. When a woman eventually succeeded in swimming the world's widest river, Dumas abandoned his project on the grounds that it "was not man's business any more," and turned his attention instead to the (considerably shorter) crossing of the English Channel, where he failed yet again.

It was on the rebound from his Channel-swimming efforts that Dumas became a serious sailor. In France he bought a boat which he named *Lehg*, and he sailed across the Atlantic from Arcachon to Buenos Aires, a newsworthy feat in those days, and one that earned Dumas the enmity of the Buenos Aires Yacht Club establishment, for his Atlantic passage narrowly scooped the club's own transatlantic venture.

This world of international swimming and yachting would not ordinarily have been open to the near-penniless son of a tailor, but Dumas was supported by the shadowy figure of his mistress, for whom he left his wife and children in 1931—the same year as his first voyage. (Faithful after his own fashion, he returned to his wife twenty years later.) All I know of the mistress—which is all that Ricardo Cufré, Dumas's Argentinian biographer, chooses to reveal—is that, in Cufré's words, "the initials of this lady's name and surname form the word *Lehg*." L.E.H.G. owned a country property outside Buenos Aires, and here, when he was not off sailing, Dumas worked on the land as a farmer and horse breeder.

Dumas the artist and Dumas the athlete combined to conceive his circumnavigation of 1942–43. On the one hand, it would be a great headline-grabbing stunt. On the other, it would be an eloquently peaceful, private gesture in a world at war. Argentina was a neutral power, though the Castillo government was packed with Nazi sympathizers. Vito Dumas was apolitical, so far as one can tell, but his route took him to the

Allied strongholds of South Africa and New Zealand, where he made friends among the troops and generally played the part of unofficial peace ambassador from a suspect country. The route itself was largely dictated by the war. Had Dumas ventured any farther north, he would have found himself entangled in the battles that were being fought on the Atlantic and Pacific; whatever its other disadvantages, the wild Southern Ocean was a region of relative calm in World War II. The picture of a small boat, with one prayerful man aboard, making its quiet way around the globe, while most of the watery world was infested with gunfire and torpedos, is a haunting one, and Dumas was fully aware of its wider significance. He meant by his example to show that all "was not lost after all, that dreamers propelled by their inward vision still lived, that romance somehow managed to survive."

Art shapes life to fit the composition, and in the opening chapters of *Alone through the Roaring Forties* Dumas the romantic artist takes some liberties with the facts of his own life. The tailor's son slyly alludes to his likely descent from the Italian aristocracy, and deftly represents himself as half country gentleman, half city dandy, loafing at leisure with his luncheon guests, his athletic club, his newspapers, and that manicurist—even as he confesses to penury. In fact, penury was much closer to the truth: *Lehg II* was set afloat largely by the generosity of the Italian-speaking waterfront community in Buenos Aires, who donated many hours of free labor, along with food parcels and clothing for the indigent voyager. Yet for his book Dumas needed to cast himself as a figure whose life of indulgent privilege on land would stand in sharp contrast to his life at sea, and so he created this soft and pampered alter ego—the lazy aristo (he might be Bertie Wooster's Argentinian cousin) who is suddenly moved by the war to do something useful, unexpected, and spectacular. Perhaps he was recalling passages from his life with Ms.

G., who appears to have receded from the picture by the time that Dumas made his famous voyage. At any rate, this somewhat uneasy mingling of images of poverty and grandeur does reveal how Dumas, from the outset, saw his book as a kind of parable in which an Argentinian socialite would be taught a great and humbling lesson by the ocean.

At sea, Dumas is born again. The early pages of the book are cluttered with references to childhood. "I seemed to be returning to infancy" is how he describes his 1937 capsize; delayed by bad weather, "I felt like a very frustrated orphan;" at the Plaza de la Libertad, "I saw myself in my far-off childhood, running or driving in a tiny carriage drawn by two lambs;" when he weeps, "I reverted to childhood;" when his old seaman's knife, long used on the farm, is restored to his seabag, "The seaman was being reborn in the bag." We're meant to understand that when, at last, *Lehg II* is unmoored from her berth in Montevideo and sets sail for Cape Town, Dumas is leaving his old, grown-up self behind; in a world contaminated by war, the sea returns him to a state of enchanted innocence.

Innocence is the book's hallmark. Though one never loses sight of the fact that Dumas was an immensely skilled seaman and navigator—and tough as old boots—his writing preserves a great deal of the perpetual eight-year-old who lives inside us all. "There is a state of mind, peculiar to the sailor, which is simple and human because it does not deal in subtleties," he says, confessing that he has "heard many voices at sea accompanied by the sound of bells." Dumas's great achievement in this book is his re-creation on the page of that state of mind, and state of wonder, which sailors share with watchful children.

Every lonely single-hander has adopted a pet creature for want of more responsive company: Slocum had his dolphin (the iridescent fish, not the mammal); Chichester had his pigeon; Donald Crowhurst had Desmond the Doddery Dorado. But in the curious bestiary of sea companions, Dumas's fly surely takes the red rosette:

> As a good host I offered it some sugar; it buzzed around and then perched on my hand. . . . . It was a well-brought-up fly, not one of those impertinent creatures who, out of all the available resting places, chooses your nose; so I took care of it. It was my traveling companion, a good friend who kept me entertained and thus repaid my trouble.

There is—miraculously—no whimsy here. You believe Dumas when he says that the fly kept him entertained, just as you believe him when he gate-crashes a "committee" of ten albatrosses, sitting on the water in a circle,

> their beaks directed to a central point which they were examining with interest. As I got nearer, I saw that the object under discussion was a small jar. They sounded rather like ducks, but with a deeper pitch, and seemed to be holding a conference on this inedible object.

The childlike gravity of Dumas's tone, along with his observant eye, save passages like these from being merely cute. And, unlike the animal encounters in Slocum, Chichester, Crowhurst, et al., they come across as the natural response to solitude of an eminently warm-hearted man who was prepared to take his company as he found it. Dumas was happy to talk to a fly if the fly was the only fellow creature available for conversation, but there's no suggestion (as there is in so many books by single-handers) that he was learning to prefer the companionship of flies to that of men and women, or that he had somehow himself become a creature in the world of Nature.

For Dumas is the sanest of all the solo voyagers. No one else sustains such a fine and reasonable balance between the call of solitude and the need for society. His moments of serene contentment alone at sea (and they are many) are achieved because the pleasures of the land are always in his mind, and he enjoys himself extravagantly on land because the lonely ocean is never more than a few days away. Sailing without a radio (carrying one in wartime would have labeled him a spy), Dumas instead calls up St. Teresa when he's in need of help, and she seems to come through a good deal more reliably than any marine operator of that period. The sight of a woman's pink silk slipper, with a pompom, floating on the waves makes him almost as happy as if the woman herself had appeared, walking on water. Even crossing the Greenwich meridian cheers him, not because it is a measure of distance traveled, but because it is a sign of "human life." Alone on the remotest patch of ocean, Dumas has the knack of conjuring around himself the comforts of a social whirl.

He is no less adept on land. During his three weeks in Cape Town, he manages to have an idyllic affair with a woman (and, or so he says, with no hard feelings afterward). In New Zealand, he becomes an adopted member of an affectionate family. When not being a lover, or a son, Dumas is to be found making new friends in bars. His chosen motto, "Never let a friend's hand grow warm in yours," sounds heartless, but Dumas sees in it the recipe for human happiness, and so long, at least, as you are reading his book, you're inclined to believe him.

Other solo circumnavigators have made the world seem dauntingly larger by their harrowing exploits; Dumas makes it smaller. He rides lightly over the vicissitudes of his voyage, perhaps because his mission was to connect up the world at a time when it was tragically divided. Nothing becomes him so well (or so nicely expresses the essential message of his voyage) as his elegant and witty handling of the apartheid system of South Africa:

> A bar, run by an Englishman who talked only with one side of his mouth and smiled with only half his face (probably so that the other half should not know), displayed the same sign

["Reserved for Europeans"]. But . . . the most curious circumstance is that adjoining this bar was another, identical in form
and decoration, communicating with the first by a door situated behind the barman. One place was for whites, the other
for blacks. Two halves of bar, two halves of expression . . .

I was never able to determine which side caught the barman's
smile and which his straight face.

It's hard to imagine a more compact deconstruction of the
absurdities of apartheid, yet Dumas carries it off with a supreme
lightness of tone. He is himself the polar opposite of that two-
faced barman. In his book, he reunites the sea and the land, and
circles the globe in order to befriend everyone he meets. In the
grim context of 1942–43, Dumas's voyage seems to shine like
the proverbial good deed in a naughty world.

THE PHOTOGRAPH OF DUMAS'S RECEPTION in Buenos Aires in September 1943 (page 162) tells its own story: at a time when
Argentina had little to be proud of, Vito Dumas was a great
national hero. Unfortunately, national heroes are always useful
tools for ambitious politicians, and Dumas's arrival in B.A. happened to coincide with the inexorable rise of the dictator Juan
Perón, who was then head of the Secretariat of Labor and Social
Welfare in the newly formed provisional government of General Pedro Ramirez. Perón, already shaping his national-socialist
program for Argentina, saw Dumas as the perfect poster child for
his coming regime. Evidently Perón paid scant attention to
Dumas's notion of himself as an aristocratic landowner: he—
quite correctly—identified the sailor as an authentic hero of the
Argentinian working class who had risen to fame against all the
odds on his native talents. In Perón's New Argentina, the hered-
itary elite (usefully represented by the B.A. Yacht Club) were to
be cut down, and the Dumases of the world were to be set free
from their chains.

Perón eventually became president in June 1946. He showered Dumas with favors, giving him a naval pension with the rank of lieutenant (which greatly annoyed the naval establishment), putting his head on a postage stamp, and establishing him as director of the Perón Nautical School. A street in the city now bears his name; so does the maritime museum.

There appears to be no record of Dumas ever speaking on behalf of the Perón regime, but after the dictator's fall, Dumas was tainted by association, and the old order bit back. According to Ricardo Cufré, "they tried to scratch his name from history." In *Alone through the Roaring Forties*, Dumas's innocence of spirit served him wonderfully well; in his dealings with Perón, one wishes he had shown himself to be capable of a little more guile.

THE VITO DUMAS of *Alone through the Roaring Forties* is a joy to meet. Who else would finish a book about his own historic circumnavigation with a touching prayer for the peace and safety of other people, at sea and on land? He speaks from the page with the compelling authority of a good, kind, and simple man who has encircled a mad world.

That, though, is not quite how he appeared in life. Ricardo Cufré, his biographer, is an ardent admirer of Dumas, and has himself sailed a catamaran along much of Dumas's Roaring Forties route. Cufré writes of his "obsessive," "demanding," "pathological" personality, and describes him as "an eternal chaser of triumphs." "It was not easy to be around him. I have talked with people who sailed with him, and they tell me that he was very taciturn, he hardly spoke on board."

This is strikingly at odds with the character to be encountered in the book—a figure of saintly amiability who appears to be miraculously free of the obsessive traits usually associated with famous single-handers. Reading Francis Chichester, for instance, you catch a whiff of brimstone in his makeup, and there are several moments in Slocum to remind you that he could be a cantankerous old rogue. Fascinatingly, Dumas never betrays egotism or worldly ambitiousness. Taciturn? He is the most confiding of men—between the covers of his book, at least.

We shouldn't be surprised. Books often mirror what is best and most generous in the character of their writers, and clearly *Alone through the Roaring Forties* gives us the best of Vito Dumas. His voyage, in any case, was a great original. It was the partial inspiration for Chichester's circumnavigation in *Gipsy Moth IV*, which begat the Golden Globe Race of 1968–69, which begat. . . . The ghost of Vito Dumas hovers over a Southern Ocean that is now continuously streaked with the wakes of solo around-the-worlders; a modest, kindly ghost, clad in burlap underwear, saying his prayers, and talking to flies.

I am most grateful to Ricardo Cufré for letting me see a copy of his and Roberto Alonso's book, Vito Dumas: Testimonio de la Leyenda, *and for dealing patiently and at length with my questions about Dumas. Since I cannot read Spanish, our communications had to be relayed through a third party; Carlos Reynales kindly agreed to read Cufré's and Alonso's book for me, and to translate our correspondence. Many thanks to him for his lively and engaged discussion of the issues raised by the book.*

All direct quotations attributed to Cufré in my introduction are from a letter to me dated 12 April 2001.

NAVAL ATTACHÉ
BRITISH EMBASSY
BUENOS AIRES

RECEPTION IN HONOUR OF VITO DUMAS

Thursday, the 12th of August at 13.00 hours in the English Club, Calle 25 de Mayo 586, Buenos Aires.

Speech by the Naval Attaché of the British Embassy, Captain H. A. Forster, R.N.

"I have the honour to communicate the following message of congratulation from the Royal Cruising Club of London on the occasion of your magnificent feat.

It reads:
'To Vito Dumas, Yacht Club, Buenos Aires. Commodore, officers and members of the Royal Cruising Club, London, have learnt with great interest that you have arrived at Buenos Aires after lone circumnavigation of world via Cape of Good Hope, Australia and Cape Horn and send warmest congratulations on your magnificent feat of skill and endurance.' "

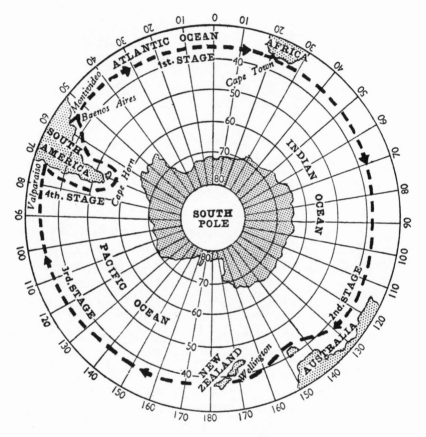

Map of route taken by Vito Dumas in his single-handed
voyage round the world.

TRANSLATOR'S FOREWORD

THE MOST ASTONISHING THING about this book—as distinct from the feat which it records—is that it should have escaped translation into English long enough for the honour to fall upon me.

Vito Dumas was born in Buenos Aires on September 26th 1900. A keen swimmer from early youth, he won the championship of the River Plate when he was 23 by crossing 42 km. of this estuary, noted for its strong currents, from Colonia (Uruguay) to the Argentine coast, remaining 25½ hours in the water. At the same time he conceived an affection for such sailing in small boats as is always within reach of a tough, willing and handy youngster. These trips afforded him an escape from the worries of a rather straitened family life and it is not difficult to understand how the sea came to be identified in his mind with freedom and the great peace of solitude.

Apart from his voyages and some short periods in Spain and France, Vito Dumas has always lived in the Argentine, ranching and farming until, time after time, the insistent call to the loneliness, beauty and danger of the sea became irresistible.

All his boats with the exception of *Lehg I*, built in France, have been designed and built in the Argentine. His ocean voyages began in 1931 with the crossing from Arcachon to Buenos Aires in *Lehg I*—a distance of 6,270 nautical miles in 74 days' sailing. His boat, an old international 8-metre, had some twenty years in her timbers. Dumas was the first to make an ocean crossing in this type of boat; Alain Gerbault's comment was that he never would have attempted it. Nevertheless it was the *Dorade*, an American built yawl, that won the transatlantic race the same year and her lines were of racing yacht rather than of the conventional types regarded at the time as the most seaworthy.

It was in 1942 that Dumas embarked on the unprecedented cruise of which he tells in this book. The moment chosen for this splendid gesture may not have been quite fortuitous; in those dark days the Swastika was within striking distance of Cairo and Moscow, and the Rising Sun, of Queensland. Perfectly aware of the dangers and hardships confronting him, he flung his gauntlet in the teeth of Fate and, with an Apostolic trust in God and a well-found ship, he set out without wireless, without funds or a spare oilskin.

Dumas's voyage may be summarized briefly as follows:

He left Buenos Aires on the 27th of June 1942 and reached Cape Town on the 25th of August—55 days to cover 4,200 miles. A ghastly misadventure at the beginning of the run very nearly terminated his career. He remained only three weeks in Cape Town before starting on the next leg of his journey, which proved to be the worst; 7,400 miles to Wellington in 104 days. After a month's very necessary rest, he was off again on the 30th January 1943. The passage to Valparaiso, which he reached on the 12th of April, was uneventful compared to the other stages of the journey. Dumas lingered there deliberately until the 30th of May, waiting for the crucial moment to tackle his last and most formidible adversary, Cape Horn.

This satanic region has been too well described to require any comment here. Having rounded the Cape with a degree of luck which his judgment and determination had most fully deserved, he reached Mar del Plate on the 7th of July 1943, 37 days and 3,200 miles from Valparaiso. He had made some remarkable daily runs, averaging 120 miles at times, and had even attained 175 miles in twenty-four hours. To achieve this single-handed in a 31 foot-overall yacht is a performance which has been equalled by few fully manned racers of similar size.

His landfalls in the River Plate on the outward and return journey may be discounted; he had circumnavigated the globe with three landfalls in twelve and a half months, of which 272 days were spent at sea; he had sailed 20,420 miles, staying close to the ill-omened 40° parallel. In so doing he broke four records: he was the first lone navigator to round the Horn and survive, Al Hansen having been wrecked shortly after his success; the first lone navigator to round the Horn from West to East; the first— and we may expect the last-to take the "impossible" route he chose; and the only one to have sailed round the globe with only three landfalls. Anyone ambitious to emulate let alone surpass him can lay claim to a head as well as a heart of oak.

The impossible has been proved possible *once*—by one very tough, gallant and experienced sailor, who on top of these qualities enjoyed a generous hand-out of luck. That should suffice. As Dumas himself says: "Never, never again."

But he was by no means finished with ocean voyaging. In 1945 *Lehg II* and her skipper sailed on the 1st of September to Buenos Aires, and after calls in South America set out for Havana, arriving there on the 9th of March 1946 after a run of 5,400 miles from Rio de Janeiro. After leaving Havana on the 2nd of June, *Lehg II* appears to have taken the bit between her teeth, for they passed New York, the Azores, Madeira, the Canaries and the Cape Verde Islands without stopping, to call at Ceará, Brazil, on the 16th of September, having spent 106 days at sea and covered 7,000 miles without a landfall. From first to last this 17,045 mile cruise took 234 sailing days.

No doubt he was at a loss to find some new problem, for it was not until 1955 that he set out for New York from Buenos Aires in a boat of 2½ tons displacement, the *Sirio*. With one landfall, at Bermuda, he sailed 7,100 miles in 117 days.

So it is not surprising that in June 1957 Dumas received the following letter:

> "I am very pleased to inform you that the Slocum Prize has been conferred on you by a vote of the members of the Slocum Society. It is normally to be given for the most remarkable trans-oceanic crossing achieved during the previous year, but on this occasion we have made an exception to the rule to honour the extraordinary voyages made by the greatest solitary navigator in the world.
>
> "Will you accept my congratulations on being the first to receive the Slocum Prize? With this prize, which we now send you, we do homage to yourself and to the great captain from whom it takes its name. In spite of its small intrinsic value, I hope that you will have much pleasure in receiving it as we ourselves have in conferring it on you."
>
> (Signed) RICHARD GORDON MACCLOSKEY,
> *Secretary.*

MANY YACHTSMEN have attended many distributions of prizes, cups, medals and trophies; they know how soon the memory of minor prowesses fades like fire in stubble once the freshness of the event and the euphoria of commemoration are past. This is something different. Deeds of quite exceptional skill and courage, involving weeks and months of solitary hardship, have, on due deliberation, been found superior to anything previously known and rewarded on that basis. The Slocum Prize is an Order of Merit which Dumas undoubtedly deserved. For though many since Slocum's time have sailed great distances in small craft, most of them have followed prudently in the well-buoyed channels of previous experience. Dumas had the vision of a Michelangelo to foresee the unforeseeable and accomplish the impossible.

And, like the cosmic artists of the Renaissance, his activities spread over many fields. He is not only a musician but a painter, whose pictures have that transparency, depth of feeling and rhythm which the ocean demands and which those who know it can best appreciate.

All this—and farming too!

Like all original and versatile artists, he has very definite ideas and some of his idiosyncrasies may be criticized. He himself knows best why he dispenses with a sea anchor or a bilge pump. One may well ask why he never caught fish or why *Lehg II* carried only one screwdriver. Never mind: he is justified by faith and works; and the "dear little cherub that sits up aloft" watched over him.

And if he is determined to die with his sea boots on, I venture to suggest that he should call his boat *La Santita*.

I am indebted to Viscount Traprain, Mr. William Mason and Mr. D. H. Shackles, C.B.E. for their very kind assistance on certain technical points.

RAYMOND JOHNES

Barometer readings in this book are expressed in millimetres.
100 millimetres = 3.94 inches.

INTRODUCTION

FOR A LONG TIME I dreamt of finding a seaman among my ancestors—a pirate, a "black ivory" merchant; at the very least someone from a romantic seaport in lovely Brittany. No luck: nothing but landsmen. At the time of the Revolution our great-grandfather was a prelate who escaped the massacres, took refuge in a little village in Italy, became a teacher and got married. No doubt he avoided the subject of his past; this, and the fact that many records were destroyed at that time, has made it impossible for us to trace farther back. All that I can add is that the portrait of General Dumas which was shown in the Arts pavilion of the Colonial Exhibition struck me by its remarkable resemblance to my father and my uncles.

But there was nothing of the sailor in this general's life, nor yet in his descendants: one was a Cavalière of the Order of the Crown of Italy; another, the only sporting one, set up a world motor-cycle speed record in 1910.

Where did I get my love of the sea?

Conspicuous among the memories of my youth are the expeditions we used to make with my father. He took us into the country or to Buenos Aires, especially into the La Boca quarter among the Genoese who could not bear to part from their ships, and so cast anchor there. On those calm Sundays I was impressed by the great masts of the sailing ships, the apparently inextricable tangle of rigging; but I cannot say that this sight gave me any

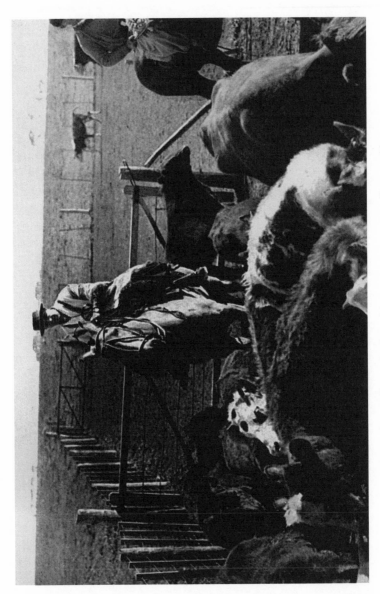

The Author on horse-back on his country estate near Buenos Aires.

Lehg II being painted and re-fitted at the Argentine Yacht Club
before departure.

very definite ideas on my own future: it was too far away. And though I loved to read tales of pirates and musketeers, I did not feel a serious call to either of these professions.

But I shall never forget the shock experienced in the little library that provided me with intellectual nourishment, when I was told:

"But you've read them *all*!"

When vacation time came round we used to go to the seaside, and we went by sea. Unfortunately the trip took place by night and thus the longed-for contact with the ocean meant no more than a visit to the ice-cream merchant on board, after which my father sent me off to bed. No, those trips can hardly be counted as sea voyages.

Yet one night I noticed that the passengers were not walking normally; they moved about hesitantly and unsteadily. This was something I failed to understand, so I asked for an explanation.

My mother, fearing that I might be feeling sick, replied with her usual gentleness:

"Don't worry about that, dear; it's because they don't feel well."

"But why do they travel if they're not feeling well?"

That was my youthful reaction. At no time in my seafaring life have I ever experienced that very common type of suffering.

It must be a great disappointment to those who would like to see in me a reincarnation of some sailor longing to return to his element. No. And I never dreamt of exploring fabulous countries either.

The fine care-free years of my life were spent in the fields, and I know them well. Then came hard times of work, struggle and worry—hardship that became a physical experience. I was only 14 years old when I came to understand what my parents felt as their resources dwindled to the point of hunger. Meals were reserved for my brother and me. So I decided to leave my books and go to work. I pretended to my parents that I had had enough of school; they understood that I was aware of the situation and made no comment.

So my new life in long trousers began; one more man took up the struggle for existence. Neither a pirate nor a musketeer, I embarked on the most commonplace task—washing floors, running errands, polishing brass for a wholesale business. A long way from my distinguished ancestor at the Italian Court!

My former schoolmates seldom missed the opportunity of calling out: "Look at him; he's working!" with a hearty laugh that was meant to be offensive. It didn't hurt. It was a shock, of course, but I never felt bitter. My feelings were very mixed—a kind of savage satisfaction that I was not the only sufferer from poverty, and a secret exaltation that made light of misunderstandings. This last may be called optimism; it has always protected me from the hard knocks of life. And although I was not quite indifferent to the attitude of former classmates who came to jeer at me as I polished the brasses, the sorrows of my first month at work were amply repaid by the joy of my parents when I brought back the little handful of pesos I had earned.

Then I got organized. In the daytime I worked; in the evenings I went to the Academy of Art to study drawing and sculpture. Still nothing in the least nautical. . . .

I shall tell elsewhere of the train of circumstances which brought me back from France, alone on board the *Lehg I*, setting my course on the Southern Cross. How far away it seems, that evening in 1931 when the sun was gilding the dunes of Arcachon as I set out! Misty, too, my successes—triumphal entries into Vigo, the Canaries, Rio Grande do Sul, Montevideo and, finally, Buenos Aires. Today *Lehg I* rests in the Lujan Museum. And how times have changed!

WAR . . .

A breath of panic ran round the world. It seemed that all was lost.

All I had to do was to stay quiet. It's so easy and comfortable, and routine presses on the shoulders of whosoever would rise from his seat and go.

Nevertheless, what did I do at home on rainy days? Bending over my charts, in spirit I was on the seas. I was studying the Roaring Forties: the "impossible route."

What set me off, to throw off all my normal life and tempt fate? Was it to show that I was not lost after all, that dreamers propelled by their inward vision still lived, that romance somehow managed to survive? The young need examples; maybe, without being too self-conscious, I could provide one. I was torn between two alternatives: to stay, to lunch at a given hour, to wait for someone, receive guests, read newspapers, and tattle with friends outside working hours: the clock would go on telling the hours and I should be one of those creatures chained to the treadmill of today and tomorrow. Or else—more generous and perhaps even more altruistic—to respond to that appeal which John Masefield expresses so well in "Sea Fever."

My decision was made, the first step taken. Nothing would stop me now; I had only to say "goodbye," perhaps forever. Before me lay the unknown of the "impossible" seas. My charts, the apparatus of navigation, the chronometer, the old compass, the tables—all those loved objects I had kept would go to sea again with me. And so my life as a sailor began once more.

ONE

THE SEARCH FOR A MATE

ON THIS ENTERPRISE a mate was obviously necessary—that is, the boat.

It had to be *Lehg II*, which I had built in 1934 with the idea of sailing around the world. But difficulties had mounted up and, apart from a few trial runs and pleasure cruises, I always returned to the land; pushing a plough seemed to put my dreams to sleep. The seafaring vagabond was getting stuck in the furrows. I sold my boat to buy a tractor, thus putting one ideal in the place of another—less romantic, admittedly, but still an ideal. And in spite of the digs that a sailor's conscience gave me, I had given up the idea of seeing *Lehg II* again. I made real efforts to forget the sea and cling to the land; the earth to which I even dedicated long, secret poems. The sea was so far away that I could hear its voice only in my imagination; yet sometimes, standing on a hill, I sniffed the wind that had passed over the vast estuary of the River Plate; it smelt different from the breeze of the pampas, it had a different quality. But the earth had got such a hold on me that one day, when a woman remarked how wonderful it must feel to be alone on the sea, I replied:

"Man was born into society and he must return."

Yet that evening, I thought of my "mate." I felt I had to find her and see her again.

On the morning on which I left the *campo*, courage failed me after the cordial farewells of the peons. I could not turn back to look at the horses, the plough, the little tree that grew on the stark plain, thanks to my parental care—not even to say goodbye to my dog Aramis. I got into my car and drove to the ring-fence; looking back I saw that the dust of my passing had obscured the tangible certainties behind me; in front lay incalculable hazard.

The whitewash I had put on the fence some time back had stood the weather well. This little detail gave me some pleasure and I almost stopped thinking; but the dust was settling and soon the familiar landscape would be visible. I felt the danger of finding myself back on that dusty road; and with something akin to fear I averted my eyes and slammed the gate.

My kitbag was sitting beside me in the car. In it were the old oilskin that I bought in France for my first voyage, sailmaker's needles and thread, even signal flares. Some of them had been used as fireworks on *fiesta* evenings in the country. The others were returning to the sea in that kitbag that forms part of the sailor; they might be used sometime, with nothing to celebrate. My dear old seaman's knife was there too; in the *campo* I had used it for cutting up meat. Now it was going back proudly to its proper use. The seaman was being reborn in the bag.

Many thoughts were passing through my head to the purr of the engine. A saying came back to me: "Never let a friend's hand get warm in yours." One must always say "goodbye" and pass on. So I must start again saying goodbye to all things—ports, towns, human contacts. The hands of my friends should not get warm in mine, I would not give them time; I would carry the warmth of friendship with me into endless solitude.

The bag did not feel at home in the car. It wanted to go back where it belonged—in the cabin of *Lehg II*. But where, oh where, was the boat?

Dr. Raphal Gamba, to whom I had sold her, still owned her. I took my brother Remo and sought him out.

It was all quite clear: I needed just that boat and no other. It would take too long, perhaps a year, to have a new one built. I could not delay my departure for the favourable season was near, and besides that, now that my decision had been made, something had started up inside me. We discussed a jumble of figures and dreams. The boat was put on the slip and the Argentine Yacht Club offered to stand the expense of making her seaworthy. Manuel M. Campos, the naval architect who supervised the repairs, designed masts and sails to stand up to the terrible seas where I was bound. My old friends the Russo brothers of La Boca, artists in their own way, made the sails without asking how and when they were going to be paid for time and materials. They had no illusions; for them to contribute their bit to the enterprise was enough.

"We're not in the habit of keeping ships waiting," they said. And everybody worked without unnecessary words.

I was going to leave a lot of debts behind me without a clue as to who was going to pay them. Fortunately my old Fencing and Gymnastic Club in Buenos Aires wanted to help me; they paid for the sails. So that was all right and so were the repairs. Only one tiny problem remained: I had not enough money to pay for the boat. I had hoped to raise the money by selling a batch of cattle; but the unfortunate beasts, having been driven from the ranch to one remote fair and then another, were so weak and thin that they could hardly walk. The irony of it! I had sold *Lehg II* to buy a tractor and I could not sell enough cows to buy her back.

"I'm told that cattle don't sell," I said to Arnold Buzzi; "they're going to die on their feet."

"I was always against your scheme," he replied, "but since you've made up your mind, leave the cows in peace to fatten up. Here's the money you need for the boat."

Furthermore, I had the invaluable collaboration of the members of the Buchardo Club, nicknamed "slavers." They worked incessantly on *Lehg II* for the fun of it. They brought their own maté and biscuits; they drove in a nail and had a sip of maté; a screw and another maté. Laughing, always laughing at their work, for which time was of no account. I cannot express the value of their work to me and can never forget it.

The water tanks aboard were inadequate; but time passed and I could not linger over every detail. Here another friend materialized, Innocencio of Lower Belgrano. He was a small shopkeeper, and he left shopkeeping to his wife while he trotted round the town pricing tanks. I also needed tins for sea biscuits. Innocencio dumped out his goods in bulk, took the tins and soldered them up himself. It was high time for my preparations to finish; Innocencio was on the point of losing his business—and his wife, who had had enough of running it single-handed.

One day he said confidentially:

"You're going to some very cold parts—you'll need hard liquor."

"Can't do much about that," I replied, "look what it costs."

Innocencio found the answer. He persuaded a number of his clients to present me with a few bottles each, and so I got an excellent advertisement combined with a fine cellar; they were very useful.

Thanks to the kindness of my friends, I acquired everything I needed as the time for departure got nearer. For example, a photographer from *El Grafico* called on me one day with a request from his director for a picture of me in a fur hat and gloves.

"I'm quite willing," I replied, "but I haven't any."

"Never mind," said he, "I'll bring them tomorrow."

The fur cap might have been made for me and the gloves were magnificent. The photograph was taken. I wrote a note to the proprietor of the magazine, saying: "Dear Gaston: This is just the job: very many thanks;" and I kept the cap and gloves.

And what a piece of luck to meet my friend Bardin. I went to see him to have a talk . . . and next day I had a complete ship's medicine chest. My doctor friends gave me ampoules of antibiotics, adrenalin, caffeine injections, etc. Everyone brought me little boxes labelled "Medical Samples. Not to be sold." The law could rest easy: they sold me nothing.

On one evening I spent with the "Banda di Estribor," Professor Niceto Loizaga expatiated on the dangers of scurvy for navigators. Of course I knew of this sort of organic decomposition which can attack anyone deprived of fresh foods for sixty days. Would I be a victim of the scourge of old-time seamen? With vitamins I should be safe enough: but how to buy them? A few days later quantities of vitamins A, B_1, C, D and K arrived on board, together with a mound of glucose to keep my calories up to standard.

My friend Corteletti was working on another line. One day I received 400 bottles of sterilized milk and a quantity of chocolate milk that would keep for a year; all this from the stocks of the Argentine Yacht Club. Another surprise was six tins of cocoa, 20 kilos of lentil flour, split peas, chick peas, 10 kilos of maté, cans of oil and 10 kilos of corned beef. Then came quantities of chocolate of every kind, fifteen tins of condensed milk, 70 kilos of potatoes, ten jars of jam, cigarettes, pipe tobacco, and what have you. I began to wonder whether I was going to sea or starting a business.

On my last day my friend Scotto gave me a log to measure the distance travelled—and I don't know how many boxes of matches. Finally, all I had to buy in this land of corn was—biscuits!

"What do you propose to wear when it rains?" asked Señor Llavallol in the course of a friendly visit.

"A raincoat."

He burst out laughing and gave me a note for a store; I went there and came out fully equipped.

I shall never forget when my friend Weber came to see me. Rather awkwardly he drew me aside and showed me a fine woolen dressing-gown. He didn't want to hurt my feelings—and I had not so much as an overcoat. Weber could not imagine the pleasure he was giving me. Another very useful gift, from Dr. Torres, was a pair of thick socks knitted by his wife. I wore them so much that I had to darn them with sail thread. For it must not be forgotten that all my ports of call were subjected to wartime rationing and that I could not replace clothing.

Enrique Tiraboschi gave me a leather jerkin. He was an optimist. Praising the garment, he told me to take great care of it, not to get it crumpled or scratched, because I would not feel the cold when I wore it. In fact, I needed this magnificent jerkin—with five or six woolies underneath, two sets of oilskins on top and a thick layer of newspaper next my skin to keep out the polar winds.

Everything aboard had to be stowed so that I could keep an eye on it and that it should not come adrift in the rolling and pitching of the boat. In this respect my worst fears were more than justified. Several times I was on my beam ends in a way I should never have believed possible.

The date of my departure was set for the 26th of June.

TWO

MY FAITH IN LEHG II

THE BOAT WAS OF THE BUILD known in France as a "Norwegian with pointed stern," in Spanish a "double prow." Length 31 ft. 6 in., beam 10 ft. 10 in., draught fully laden 5 ft. 8 in., a cast-iron keel weighing 7,700 lb. Apart from provisions I carried 90 gallons of water in two tanks and 21 gallons of kerosene for cooking and lighting. I could stay at sea for a year without revictualling.

Lehg II was ketch rigged, that is to say with a mainmast and a mizzen. The mainmast was one made in France for *Lehg I* in 1913. It was therefore thirty years old at the start of my voyage. The suit of sails comprised jib, storm jib, mainsail and mizzen. I carried a complete set of spares, plus a storm trysail and an enormous balloon jib for very light weather. The cabin top was permanently covered with canvas to prevent the waves from beating continuously on it, starting the seams and causing leaks. Furthermore it kept the cabin in twilight, so that I could sleep in the daytime.

I had not forgotten a spare tiller. My provisions were complete: nothing was left to chance. If I did not succeed it would not be from lack of foresight; on this sort of enterprise there is no room for improvisations. Everything must be calculated and measured.

I knew how well my boat could behave in heavy weather on the high seas. In 1937, on a trip to Rio de Janeiro, I was surprised by a *pampero* squall blowing at between 60 and 70 knots—

7

the one which wrecked the *Bonny Joan*[†] and *Shaheen* on the rocks of the Punta del Este. As for myself, I was in the area where the *Cachalot* vanished without trace.

It was in the evening. I was making myself some chocolate and hoping to spend as pleasant a night as possible. The wind outside was so violent that a sail had been blown to ribbons, and the raging seas were something to shudder at. I was hove to, close to the wind.

Suddenly there was a terrific crash. I followed the motion of the boat and found myself sitting on the ceiling of the cabin. This was it. For several seconds of eternity the masts were pointing to the depths and the keel skywards. The chocolate was flowing over the ceiling. I was sealed in, in the total darkness and assumed that I was sinking.

I was partly stunned and there was nothing that I could do. The end of everything. I felt hot blood running on my hands. There was no way out of the darkness and confusion, and *Lehg II*, keel in air, would soon fill and sink.

It was a coffin more than a prison. Then came resignation and I relaxed. I cannot say whether my mood was one of acceptance, thankfulness even, or a kind of reverence for death, so often defied. I left everything to fate. To struggle was quite useless; I seemed to be returning to infancy.

Then *Lehg II* slowly rolled over; and keeping pace with the movement of the boat, hope came back. As soon as it was possible I scrambled back on deck; resignation was transformed into furious energy. Everything came to life at once, muscles, brains and nerves—a torrent of vitality sweeping over me. I looked at the sea and smiled. The sea and I; face to face.

I was no longer in a coffin but on my own deck. Some distance away the dinghy drifted off, awash; but nothing mattered

---

[†]*Bonny Joan*, Norwegian 59 ft. and 41 tons. *Shaheen*, schooner 98 ft., 130 tons.

now that I could fight back with eager eyes, a heart full of hope and in possession of all my faculties. From the bottom of my soul I thanked the boat, I talked to her with endearments that fled down the howling wind.

My faith in *Lehg II* dates from then.

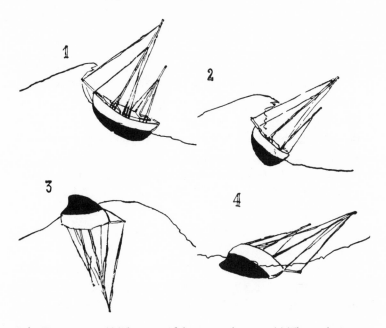

Lehg II turns over. (1) The crest of the wave advances. (2) The yacht is overwhelmed. (3) For several seconds the mast points to the depths. (4) She rights herself. The drawing records the Author's impressions and is not to scale.

THREE

GOOD LUCK

ON FRIDAY THE 26TH OF JUNE I paid my final visit to Admiral Guisasola. His aide-de-camp led me down a corridor and ushered me into a dimly lit office. Through the window behind the Admiral came a single shaft of light. Feeling a little confused by the excitement of the last few days, I tried to express myself properly and say a great many things. And all that would come out was: "Admiral, I've come to say goodbye." The words sounded hollow and I felt that it was not I who spoke. Out of the darkness came a reply:

"Good luck, Vito." And after a long silence the Admiral added: "That is what I wish you."

We embraced; and this accolade meant a great deal to me. We did not speak. Then I turned and made for the door in haste. But as I went down the corridor, rather like a clock-work dummy, a hail of good wishes followed me.

As I looked across the square from the entrance I could not pull myself together. I felt stunned, as if I had just realized what was about to happen to me. Up to then, work had kept my mind occupied; now I had to think of the voyage. The two sentries, pacing their beats, took no notice. As I walked on a policeman shook hands with me and made a "good luck" sign with his free hand.

What did I do till midnight? I don't remember. I only know that I went on like an automaton with a little spark glowing inside that told me I had finished with my friends, with fighting difficulties and correcting mistakes. I longed to feel at peace with this world that I was about to leave and that I might never find again.

For some obscure reason one scene sticks out in my memory; I see myself at midnight going aboard *Lehg II* with some friends, carrying blankets and taking a last look round.

Then I went ashore to sleep.

FOUR

THE 27TH OF JUNE

THE MORNING WAS COLD and sunny. I came out and took the Metro, and looked round at the headlines of newspapers the other passengers were reading. They said: "Dumas's duel with the sea starts today;" "Vito Dumas's return match with the sea." I was not at all awestruck; on the contrary, the fuss the press was making filled me with a kind of childish delight. People were staring at me in surprise; whispering and thinking, no doubt, that I was not dressed for the part of the lonely mariner; carrying no luggage, wearing an ordinary and quite inappropriate lounge suit, I looked like any clerk going to an office.

Getting out with the crowd at Carlos Pellegrini station, I went to the hairdresser of my Gymnastic and Fencing Club. There were still patches of white frost on the ground.

Once installed in the barber's chair, I took whatever was coming: a hot towel after the shave? Sure! Manicure? Call the girl! Shoes? I looked at them and thought a polish would do them all the good in the world. I felt like a Pasha enjoying all the pleasures of life; I surrendered to luxury. But presently the hairdresser remarked:

"So today's the day?"

I woke up. I looked at my nails that the manicurist was polishing, at my shining shoes, and asked myself what the use of it all might be. The mirror reflected my image as if to reveal me to myself. No, really, I was not "in the skin of the part," as actors say. I was not convincing my audience. Should I be serious or laugh? Should I be grave or dramatic? Not an easy part, the lonely mariner. I replied:

"Oh yes, I think so."

"But all the papers say so!" exclaimed the unfortunate man.

"If they say so it must be true."

I went on looking at myself in the mirror, making faces and trying to find one that fitted the lonely mariner, while they went on fussing over my fingernails and my shoes. It seemed to me that someone else was being titivated while the solitary navigator was looking for his face.

I lunched at the Argentine Yacht Club and had to leave the table twice to satisfy the press photographers. At 1 P.M. I started off for the boat.

Our Commodore, Señor Antonio Aguirre, was hanging round my neck, when my friend Arnoldo Buzzi drew me to one side.

"How much money have you got?"

Caramba! I hadn't thought of that one. I drew out my wallet: what Buzzi and I saw was a single 10-peso note.

"So you expect to get round the world with that?"

"Where do you expect me to spend money at sea?"

"Oh no, my dear fellow, that won't do!"

And Arnoldo, who is rather more practical than I am, gave me ten British one-pound notes.

A sailor came up to me.

"Must wish you luck, sir. I admire you. I know those seas."

"Oh, do you?"

"Yes. It was at the Cape of Good Hope that we got dismasted in a storm. Well, all I can say is that I admire you."

Nothing like encouragement, I thought. But the crowd was getting thicker. Only fifteen steps down to the dinghy that would take me to *Lehg II.*

My mother stood before me, pale and sad as I had not seen

her for many years. I don't care for family farewells; no, I never liked them. What on earth was I to say to her?

"Mother dear, smile!" I begged. "I don't want people to see you looking sad. It'll only be a year."

I kissed her and turned to go down the fifteen steps. But my brother could not restrain himself any longer; he burst into tears. He hugged me with all the vigour of despair; as I broke loose I cried:

"*Hombre!* you're suffocating me!" A childish effort to hide my feelings, to deceive him—and myself.

The crowd got thicker. I jumped into the dinghy. The last photographs, final good wishes, and handshakes, and away! I was soon on board.

Whilst I was changing, the Russo brothers and the Yacht Club hands were hoisting the sails.

Now I was alone on board. *Lehg II* was making way under the northerly breeze that had been blowing since morning. It was 13.05 hours. Behind me was the country where I was leaving my mother; she had already become, not a being of flesh and blood, but a symbol.

Two hundred yards. For the last time I looked back, scanning the prospect that stretched from the mole where the crowd had gathered to see me off, to the high wall of the Yacht Club; and throwing off the emotion I had suppressed for so many hours in order to conceal my weakness, I cried out:

"*Adios,* my country!"

I sailed slowly down the channel. To leeward, several yachts with friends were escorting me, *Angelita* leading; the Ministry of Works boats sounded their sirens as I passed.

I began to feel the sea getting choppy under the north wind. I reckoned that the run to Montevideo would not take long.

One by one my escorts dropped off. When it came to *Angelita*'s turn, whom should I see aboard but my son, Vito Diego.

I had to say something but all that came into my head was:
"Keep well! Do some good work!"

Quite simple—but something he could repeat to himself every day.

Once I was through the entrance channel of the South Basin a sloop, the last of my escort, came alongside with Arnold Buzzi, who had done a few cruises with me in the past and who was to accompany me to Montevideo. He was to see me through the congested traffic of the River Plate whilst I stowed everything that had been put aboard at the last moment.

I got down to it. Off Quilmès, Arnold sang out:
"Ship to windward!"

It was that excellent yachtsman Martinez Vasquez, the director of *El Grafico*, in his *Sea Bird*, to give me a final send-off.

I set the balloon jib to put on more speed. Darkness fell slowly; in the sunset lay Buenos Aires, which I might never see again.

Then it was quite dark; white and red, the light buoys of the channel were winking.

Ashore, the city of La Plata was a blaze of light; here and there a green light marked a wreck; ships went to and fro. On board, only the binnacle and cabin lights were shining. The wind freshened and veered to the N.E. Dinner-time went by as we chatted of this and that. Astern, the lights of La Plata were growing dimmer. I said:

"Steer E. a quarter N. while I get a little sleep. I'll take the watch at midnight."

"Right."

I lay down hoping to sleep, but without success. From time to time I would ask Arnold:

"How goes it?"

"Very well."

"Are we on course?"

"On course."

These rather futile questions were chiefly put to reassure myself that Arnold had not gone to sleep. By 1 o'clock it was no longer enough for me to ask, I had to make sure that we were on our course. Oh dear! we were heading for Mar del Plata. Arnoldo had lost his bearings. The oddest thing about it is that, once we had arrived, he thought that I made the mistake.

I decided to stay with him. We talked from time to time. The moon peered through heavy clouds. Conversation fell; silences became longer and longer.

"Do you want to sleep, Arnold?"

"Er, not much . . ."

"Right! she's keeping nicely on course, all by herself. Let's both go to sleep."

We went to bed and *Lehg II* sailed on with no one at the tiller.

As the dawn began to peer through the deadlights, I felt I must see where we were. The lie of the boat told me that the wind had freshened. Leaving Arnold asleep, I went on deck and took the tiller. Forward lay the channel buoys of Montevideo. I passed them at 8 A.M. just as Arnold was beginning to show signs of life. And at ten we anchored in the port of Buceo after some twenty hours' sailing.

This short trial trip had been useful. I had spotted several details that called for immediate attention; for example, the shrouds had got slack and the mast, no longer properly held, had taken on an alarming bend. Two sailors, friends of ours, undertook to brace them up, to change the dead-eyes for others of a more suitable size, etc.; this work being scrupulously paid for . . . with a bottle of Muscatel.

Numbers of friends came to see me, bringing welcome gifts: a seaman's knife, a picture of *Lehg I* to decorate my cabin. Another brought bottles of mineral water. Fat Mathos Puig took me in his car to a ships' chandler where I got brushes, paint, an

electric torch. Puig kept on at me till I was loaded up with a lot
of lumber I didn't know where to stow. What is certain is that the
proprietor of the shop, carried away by his eloquence, did not
allow me to pay for a thing. Everyone wanted to give me something and ask me to dinner.

For a few days a violent *pampero* caused the authorities to
close the port. I did not sleep aboard but at the Uruguayan Yacht
Club, where a red flag for danger was hoisted: the wind continued blowing at 30 knots. Nevertheless I decided to sail on July
1st. The wind and the sea were not reassuring, but I had important reasons for haste. The season of fine weather was passing and
I wanted to get to South Africa before spring.

FIVE

THE GREAT DAY

THE MORNING OF THE 1ST OF JULY was very like the preceding days; the seas were more impressive than ever.

I had arranged to start early in the afternoon; having some time to waste, I went into the centre of the town. The Avenida del 18 Julio was forbidding and full of hostile wind. I felt like a very frustrated orphan and tried to get rid of my mood by going into a bazaar and purchasing some kitchen utensils, then some newspapers which I turned over without reading them. Finally, I got into a bus to return to the club. Everyone was muffled up on this mean, cold, surly morning. We arrived at the Plaza de la Libertad, which has changed little in the course of centuries; it made me think of those quarters of Paris that remain so strikingly themselves while change goes on all round.

The Plaza de la Libertad took me back into the past; I saw myself in my far-off childhood, running or driving in a tiny carriage drawn by two lambs. O Past, why did you have to haunt me just at this moment? It often used to happen to me in the years when I was growing into manhood: suddenly I would awaken from my daydreaming and see what had been hidden. Here was the moment of truth; I had to tear myself from this spot that I had loved as a child—but beyond the years I clung to one image that had to be stored away in my innermost consciousness: my intense joy at seeing the Marqués de las Cabriolas in the Montevideo carnival and the sound of tambourines;

the procession passing under my penetrating six-year-old eyes as I sat in the little chair my parents had placed at the edge of the pavement. Now the tambourines were ringing in a sad heart that yearned back from the present to this warm, human little past.

The motor-bus went on and I woke up in front of the club.

As I ate my last lunch there, all my Uruguayan friends wanted to sit at my table in turn. They were not cheerful.

"Well, Dumas, remember that the bad weather is local; once you're away from the Uruguayan coast you will be in a calmer zone."

That was the best encouragement the Harbour Master had to offer. There was a certain amount of discussion, but many words remained unspoken.

Time was up.

The harbour was still officially closed. But I got my clearance at the Maritime Prefecture. My farewells were almost silent; I went aboard and was towed out to a mooring where it would be easier to set sail.

I set all sail. The boat was dancing; what would it be like outside? Several friends were circling round me. I slipped the mooring and *Lehg II* was quickly under way. The sou'wester was blowing at over 30 knots and the seas were heavy outside. We were soon through the harbour entrance, steering S. to avoid shoals along the coast.

The crossing to the African coast had begun; more than 4,000 sea miles. . . . I would make the acquaintance of those "roaring winds" of the forties. It was the first time that a man had ventured into them alone. What would those tomorrows bring?

For the moment I knew that my safety, my universe, depended on the security of a few planks. The only yacht that had decided to see me off in such weather was shipping heavy seas with some frequency; she went about and made for the harbour; arms were waving a last farewell.

And as this handful of friends, from a country so dear to me, drew away, I shed tears.

I needed this relief. I had choked them back too long under an outward stoicism; now I reverted to childhood.

At 16.00 hours Flores Island was abeam. I steered due East with a following wind. The sea was still rising and I could not relax my attention for a single moment. I had decided not to rest at all until I was well clear of the coast, on account of danger from congested shipping.

At 21.00 hours Iman Point, Periapolis, was abeam. The boat was bustling along as though she were under power. At 23.00 hours the pencil of light from Punta del Este was flashing at regular intervals on my sails. To the South I could see as I rose on a wave the dark mass of Seal Island.

It was a really dirty *pampero*. From time to time heavy clouds would burst in a cascade which combined with the seas breaking on deck and made it essential to batten down everything. And this went on for an entire day.

Early in the morning of the 3rd of July, dead-beat with sleepiness and fatigue in this hellish weather, I decided to take in the mainsail. I had to cling to the hand-rope and every other hold in sight. At times I had to stop work to avoid being washed overboard.

The night was still black; no sign of life anywhere. I had been on deck for forty hours without a chance to eat or drink.

The flogging of the mainsail as I lowered it made the boat quiver as if everything would break up. Finally I managed to get it lashed down and made fast.

Lehg II had lost speed and was easing up to the waves more gently. I let her lie with her head to the land. I was trembling with cold and fatigue.

Up till then I had been sailing without lights. In order to display one I entered the cabin for the first time since I set sail. What was that sound of water?

I struck a match. But my hands were numbed and stiff. I went through the whole box. It was wet: I threw it overboard. I did not know what was the matter with me: nerves or clumsiness after so many years ashore. At all events it was not till the third box that I began to be methodical. At last I got a light. And sure enough there was water in the bilge. Tired as I was, this was the last straw. . . .

The seaman must not think of himself until he has seen to the needs of his craft. So I set about baling. I must record here that never since I have been sailing have I used a bilge pump. One after another, I threw seven buckets of water over the coaming. *Lehg II* had taken all that in since Montevideo: I was surprised, as she had never made a drop of water before.

To tell the truth, I had only a vague idea of my position; I should have to pass through a good many more trials before I found my sea legs.

I had been thinking of so many things in the last few days and was so tired that I had no appetite; I only wanted to rest. I wedged myself in and went fast asleep, to awake, half-conscious, at midday. I ate a little biscuit and drank a small bottle of chocolate milk.

The weather did not mend; I decided to carry on under the staysail and mizzen. The barometer stood at 769, the thermometer at 13°C., the hygrometer at 90 per cent. No land in sight and no prospect of the wind abating. In the evening I lashed the helm and left the boat to sail herself, taking refuge in the cabin. Enormous waves came and went; *Lehg II* was groaning. From time to time a wave would crash down on the deck; the wind was now blowing at over 50 knots: I was well into the "roaring winds." I emptied twenty buckets of water; and this added greatly to the exhaustion caused by the weather.

At midnight I saw with consternation that the floor boards of the cabin were awash. At every roll the water threatened to spoil everything on board. Feverishly I tackled it and threw bucket after bucket of water overboard. I was soon exhausted. Often the bucket would empty itself over me when I had nearly got it out. I was drenched; my hands were scored and very painful. I wondered what could be happening; she had never made a drop of water before—why should she fill so quickly? Unless I could staunch the leak she would sink. I worked desperately to get all the water out so as to trace the damage, but there was a difficulty: the greater part of the space under the floor boards was filled with some five hundred bottles of assorted drinks.

In spite of the movement of the boat in the stormy seas, I had to shift all this cargo, bottle by bottle. And when I had finished I found that the leak was not where I expected.

I inspected the whole hull, from the stern to where the tins of biscuits were stowed forward and where the pitching was most violent. Passing the tins into the cabin, I hurt my hands and knocked myself about considerably. But there was the leak, at last!

There was a shake in one of the planks, which had split. This was not the time to ask how or why. Quickly I mustered a piece of canvas, red lead, putty, a piece of planking, nails and a hammer, and set about stopping the leak. I was so eager to have done and the lamp swung so violently that I kept hitting my fingers with the hammer.

At last the job was done; only a very little water was coming in; and I re-stowed all the tins.

It was four o'clock in the afternoon of the 4th of July. I had worked desperately to save the boat. But I felt the satisfaction of having overcome the first difficulty; I could now indulge in a few moments' rest.

The sea was still bad, but not quite so bad as it had been in the first days. The trouble was that everything was saturated with sea water. I went back to the helm.

The "roaring winds" were making their weight felt. The English have given them this name because, apart from their violence, they have a peculiar sound not unlike that of a saw cutting through wood. They rule the waves in 40° South, accompanied by low cloud, rain and squalls.

Dusk was falling by the time I had finished with the leak. I did a few odd jobs and looked out at the darkling sea, in the majesty of rolling waves that every now and then cut off the horizon. Stars were showing. The wind, which had touched 50 knots, had now dropped a little. Seagulls were following me and snapping up the bits of biscuit I threw to them.

When I awoke at 01.00 on the 5th of July, I saw that the light on deck had gone out; I decided not to light it again.

I proposed to organize my life as follows: in bad weather, to navigate under the staysail and mizzen and during the night to let *Lehg II* sail herself as best she might while I slept, until 7 or 8 in the morning. Such were my intentions; but an unexpected event came to modify my plans.

That morning at 8 I felt ill. My right arm was infected and there were several open wounds in my hand. I felt depressed and had not the courage to take the helm. I resolved to stay in bed.

On the 6th of July my arm was worse. The sea had gone a little, the wind remained very fresh. At 10 o'clock I set down the storm trysail, a sail for foul weather, smaller than the mainsail under which I had set out. This task, hard enough at any time on a moving deck, was doubly awkward with my right arm useless; I was beginning to get worried about the septic condition.

I remained at the helm on the look-out for a ship, but only albatrosses were to be seen. That night several porpoises, hardly breaking the surface, came to play around *Lehg II*; I was surprised to see them so far from land.

The sea became gradually calmer; for the first time the tranquil majesty of the Atlantic began to impress me. A few clouds in the sky, piling up to N.N.E. and N.N.W.

At midday on the 7th of July I took sights and got 35°47′ S. and 47° W. I was therefore 480 miles E. of Montevideo. The wind frequency chart showed that I was in the zone of twenty-four days of gales out of thirty, on an average.

And I was in a flat calm! The light breeze I hoped for was coy. The boat turned round and round, pointing most frequently to the N.E. Finally, at dusk the wind rose in the N.E. and for the first time the boat really held her course alone. My mind, too, was looking for a course and turned to J. L. Grundel, an old sea dog of the Swedish navy who had become a merchant skipper. I could see his kindly face. I fancied I heard him talking as he did shortly before I left Buenos Aires, in his precise limpid way, the words coming out like the murmur of a spring as he mourned over his seafaring past. He had remained young and strong; only on account of his "cabin boy," his son, had he renounced the sea. I remembered a great truth he had uttered in the course of one of his soliloquies: "It's out there at sea that you are really yourself." I now understood what he meant and smiled at the memory of my despair on the night when I used three boxes of matches to get a light. It is true that the beginning was the toughest, for during those first days the wind blew at times at over 50 knots, tearing out the eyelets of the canvas cover in spite of its considerable strength.

SIX

THE ARM AND THE SEA

I HAD BOTH HANDS BANDAGED and every bit of work necessary to handle the ship caused me acute pain. There was a long road ahead and I had not forgotten to ask God for guidance; but I understand also that a seaman has to suffer and that the picture one sees from ashore, when fit and well, does not include the bitter realities of life afloat. I could accept these—whilst doing my utmost not to lose altogether the illusions of happier days.

I was heading for a zone in which one storm follows another and which had never been sailed by a lone hand. I did not try to deceive myself. I knew before I started that it would not be a joy-ride; but imagination always falls short of the truth. I remembered the experiences of other navigators, but all the accounts I had read dealt with less inhospitable regions. I tried to adapt myself. I would take what was coming: I would face whatever the unknown future had in store. That evening I decided to have a feast to boost my *morale*, my first real meal since I set out. The menu: soup and fried potatoes. Not much, but for me, a banquet. So one goes on expecting less and less; and any trifle may become a source of satisfaction. Perhaps that is truly living.

The wind, which had been shifting continually, had unfortunately settled at E.S.E. on the morning of the 8th of July; I was obliged to take a tack to the S. The sky was completely overcast. I had some sleep and at 8.30 tried again to hold the tiller. As I was making no headway and getting very wet, I decided to return to the cabin, where I spent most of the time lying down. The barometer was steady at 774 and the temperature at 14°C.; wind 30 knots.

As the day went on, the weather grew worse. It began to rain and *Lehg II* sailed on alone under the storm trysail, on a south-easterly course.

During the night we had quite a shaking up. In the morning I decided to steer. At midday, when I went below to rest, I was appalled to find that there was a great deal of water in the hull. My summary efforts to master the leak had not been good enough. But the seas were too heavy for me to work on it in that part of the port bow. I should have to wait for better weather in order to make a proper job of it. But, weather permitting, would I still be able to do so? My hand, swollen and misshapen, was a nasty sight.

This hand and the whole right arm continued to swell, making movement impossible. The pain was getting worse and my temperature was rising.

In the evening I decided to give myself an injection to bring down the temperature; I spent an uneasy and feverish night in my bunk.

The next morning (10th of July) the weather was just as bad; on top of that, on this infernal course, the leak was making a great deal of water; and now I discovered that a 5 kg. jar of honey had come adrift and smashed. A disaster: the stuff had run into the bilges and made everything sticky.

Another injection. I sterilized the needle and succeeded in getting 1 c.c. of the liquid into the syringe; it was not easy to carry out this delicate operation left-handed. The jolting and banging of the boat were so continuous and so violent that I had to be very careful not to inoculate the mattress! On land, with steady hands, there is no difficulty about giving an injection, but here, nothing stayed in its place. An awkward movement, and everything was on the deck. And then—fish the needle out of the bilge, get the apparatus together and sterilize all over again. It took me a whole hour's fidgeting—in great pain, shaking with fever and sick with apprehension.

My will power had sunk to the point when, cowering in the cabin, I no longer cared whether the boat went on her course or sank. I could not sleep—for every jolt of my arm caused intolerable pain—nor think; there was only one thing in the world: my arm hurt.

The next day I gave myself another injection. The arm was monstrously swollen and my temperature never went below 40°C. I began to wonder what would happen unless I could do something more effective. I could not go on much longer like this, weak with fever, sleepless with pain.

A decision had to be made. That night must be the last with my arm in this condition. Land? I could not reach land in time. If by tomorrow things had not improved, I would have to amputate this useless arm, slung round my neck and already smelling of decay. It was dying and dragging me along with it. It was septicaemia. I could not give in without playing my last card.

There were several suppurating open wounds in the hands, but I could not localize the septic focus in this formless mass. With an axe, or my seaman's knife, at the elbow, at the shoulder, I knew not where or how, somehow I would have to amputate. I thought of the rudimentary material available for my purpose. The boat, her course, the voyage, no longer interested me. Feeble, feverish and unspeakably depressed as I was, my torments were increased by the endless rolling and pitching.

Slowly they went by, the hours of this long, long night; I yearned to sleep, to sleep for ever.

I was conscious of the inadequacy of my medical knowledge in this terrible dilemma. Amputation was the last hope, but . . . would that be a solution? Was there not a risk of complications, of a more serious and virulent reinfection?

Out of the innermost secret recesses of my soul on that unforgettable night was born a fervent prayer—my only hope. I commended myself to little St. Teresa of Lisieux; I asked her help; and I lost consciousness.

I did not know how long it was; but at about 2 o'clock in the night of the 12th of July I awoke. The bunk was damp. Could a wave breaking on deck have got in through the portholes? But I knew that they were shut tight. As I moved, my arm felt lighter. Thank God! There was a gaping hole about three inches wide in my forearm; pus was flowing from it.

With the marlinspike of my seaman's knife I tried to get out the core of the abscess. It was a sinister scene under the dying light of the swinging lamp. I was too weak to stand the revolting sight of my arm; what I did was to apply a dressing of cotton-wool with cicatrizing oil. Then I gave myself a fourth injection.

That day, as if to celebrate my recovery, the sun rose and the wind veered to S. I began mechanically to put things shipshape; mopping up the honey, disinfecting the bunk, all with my left hand. The future seemed more promising. On the 13th I went back to the tiller, which I had hardly touched for several days.

SEVEN

PREVAILING STORMS

FRESH SQUALLS BLEW UP and continued for a long time; they were characteristic of this zone of the South Atlantic.

The current was favourable. *Lehg II* was forging ahead under storm trysail, staysail and mizzen. Up to then, if the truth be told, I could not make up my mind what sail I ought to carry; I groped and experimented. In any case I could not stay on deck for long, my right arm being protected only by two dressings and a strip of material, which soon got sodden with pus. And I had to avoid getting it too wet.

The wind, which was now aft, required my constant attention and obliged me to attend to many other things apart from holding my course.

I remained at the helm until the first minutes of the 14th of July; then, as the wind did not serve to let the boat sail on her own under the amount of sail I was carrying, I lowered the storm trysail and went below for a well-earned rest. Thus *Lehg II* was heading a little into the current which, however, carried her towards the middle of the Atlantic so that, on the whole, she was on the right course.

In the morning I set the mainsail in order to make up for the delay caused by my illness. The wind was still W., blowing 30–35 knots. After drinking a bottle of chocolate and milk, I spent the day running through squalls. In the evening I was very tired and after dressing my arm—a matter which brooked no neglect—I

29

decided to leave all sail set; every two hours I got up and went on deck to check the course.

The next day I took the helm early and stayed till midday. My arm was well enough for me to shoot the sun, which gave me 36° S. 41°50′ W. So I was 720 miles E. of Montevideo. As expected, I was still in the region of gales prevailing twenty-four days a month!

In the afternoon I baled and from time to time sat down on my bunk to rest and contemplate my surroundings; they seemed quite new to me. For the first time since my departure I was happy; I felt like a guest aboard of *Lehg II*.

The barometer stood at 780 and the temperature in the cabin at 15°C. Outside the sky was strangely overcast, but I was getting used to this outlook.

Next day I was surprised to see that the glass had dropped 5 mm., while the wind had changed to N.E. overnight. The temperature rose to 17°C. Later I was to realize that when the glass falls, the wind invariably shifts to the E., which was what I needed.

One day was not like another. I decided to use the storm trysail which, although it made me lose speed when the wind was light, allowed me to proceed normally when it got fresher. It saved me some worry as well as the labour of lowering the mainsail every evening. I had made a meagre run during the last twenty-four hours, only 55 miles. The wind shifted to the N.E. which obliged me to set a course to the N.; I went on deck to carry out this manoeuvre and was glad to find everything in perfect order.

No sign of life around me except, riding the waves, a great albatross (the species whose wing spread exceeds 10 feet). Up to the present, the Pilot Chart had given me an accurate forecast of the winds; it now indicated that I was leaving the zone of unfavourable weather. I cherished the hope that kinder winds would give me better average runs. The ground swell was very heavy; huge masses of water were moving towards the N.E. My arm was much better, so I took to setting the mainsail when possible and remaining prepared to lower it immediately in case of necessity.

The hours passed in the tranquillity that comes of contemplating always the same view. The mind drifts on erratically; it jumps without pause of reason from a sentiment to a question. Why did the *Copenhagen* sink? An iceberg encountered at night, with no time to steer clear? An idea came to me—what if I met an iceberg in the night? I remembered that at this time of the year there was no thaw. Or did the *Copenhagen* meet a "white squall"—a wind that gives little notice of its arrival—which laid her on her beam ends. If she had her portholes open she could have filled and sunk to the bottom—some 2,000 fathoms hereabouts.

My thoughts wandered, hopping off hither and thither and returning without a pause for rest. It was hard for me to arrest even the memory of my mother for more than a few seconds. Everything was so strange. Yet my life on board had become quite well ordered; at night I shortened sail and went to sleep; in the morning I went back to my course and my work.

My position was 35°26' S. by 34°45' W., my speed very indifferent; some 55–65 miles a day, barely 2½ knots on an average.

The weather, which had been reasonably good for some time, got worse again. The swell was heavier and waves began to break. A wave breaking over the boat threw her on her beam ends and got into the cabin through a scuttle which I had forgotten to shut; the cockpit filled. It was really hellish weather. It was holding me back; I feared that the crossing would be a long one. I still had 900 miles to go before I got to the latitude of Tristan da Cunha. The shaking of the mizzen halyards sounded like a hammer striking an anvil. Waves were constantly breaking on board. I was sailing under the staysail and mizzen.

On the 24th the storm reached its climax; the W. wind was gusting over 70 knots. For thirty hours I kept looking astern, hoping that each blast would be the last; but the squalls followed each other continuously.

For the whole of this thirty-hour stretch I kept on humming the same song, a short catch that kept time with the endless repetition of the waves. I issued a challenge: let's see which will tire first, the weather or I. Wave after wave broke over my wretched waterlogged carcass. I chewed on a scrap of canvas impatiently. As each wave broke over me it would run down to my hand, mingle with a drop of blood and make a little pink puddle in a fold of my oilskin. But my lips still burbled on their monotonous little song; in spite of my irritation the notes came out in perfect cadence to fly down the wind.

The waves appeared over 50 feet high. They came on regularly and shot me down from their crest into the abyss. It was an infernal night; at times the black squall would close round me; and in that blackness one had to feel the wave coming, present the stern to it with a quick thrust of the tiller, then yaw back again. This game continued to the point of exhaustion.

At midnight I took advantage of a momentary lull to bring *Lehg II* up into the wind, and, leaving her to ride it out alone, I went below. The song had stopped; the weather had defeated it. I laid down on the floor of the cabin, sore and soaking wet. My hands, hardened to the cold, were no longer bleeding; they were as numbed as I was. So I spent an uneasy night, waking now and then with a start.

On the 26th of July a lull in the storm allowed me to make sail again and to mend a rent in the mizzen.

I found that in the last twenty-four hours I had made 170 miles with only the staysail and mizzen. At times I felt that the mast was coming down. But anyhow, that was over and done with, the prospects for the morrow were better and 170 miles was so much gained. I was now 1,320 miles from Montevideo; the calculation filled me with such joy that I forgave the wretched storm.

As I had taken nothing hot for several days and cherished succulent memories of my last "feast," I managed with great efforts to heat up some soup. It was marvellous.

There remained two inconveniences, which had to be borne without any enthusiasm whatever: to bale the hull twice a day and endure the accursed squalls. And then the fatigue. It was quite enough to hold the tiller and to dress my wounds at regular intervals; as a rule I did not find it necessary to add cooking to my other troubles. Instead, I flung myself into the nearest corner to sleep; the need for repose was paramount and everything seemed comfortable so long as I was not working—even the hard planking. Thus, bit by bit, all the refinements of life ashore drop away from us!

Early on the 30th the sea went down; to the E. the sky cleared and the sun shone out.

I regretted that I had no means of announcing my position to those who were awaiting my arrival in South Africa. I had not shipped a wireless transmitter because, in time of war, it might have got me into trouble.

Since my departure I had not encountered a single ship. My solitude in the Atlantic was complete except for the albatrosses and some smaller birds with pretty check patterns under their wings. These were pintado petrels or Cape pigeons. I often saw them during my long hours at the helm.

While I was throwing overboard all the stores that had been spoilt by salt water, it occurred to me that I had not heard a human voice for thirty-one days—nothing but the wind and the slap and swish of water along the hull. It was a kind of living death. My eye would seek a focal point on the enormous leaden mass of the ocean, as it always does in town or country.

Here there was nothing; and in the distance the sea itself merged with the sky.

For two days I had been running with all sail set under a southeasterly breeze and *Lehg II* kept on her course practically without attention. Night had fallen, yet at Buenos Aires it was still light; I was getting near the meridian of Greenwich. On the 3rd of August my position was 35° S. by 17°23′ W.

At last I could undertake to remove the summary repair which was letting water in, and make a better job of it. I found that the nails had rusted, causing further small leaks. I changed the tingle, put on some fresh putty and replaced the nails with screws.

I was making 105 to 115 miles every twenty-four hours. The boat was not very well balanced under sail and had a tendency to luff, which made it necessary to use quite a lot of helm to keep her on course; I felt that I should set a storm jib and this made it necessary for me to work on the end of the bowsprit.

It is common practice when embarking on this operation to make a note in the log: "Shall I get back?" Many have been carried away when indulging in this very dangerous exercise, as pitching plunges the bowsprit and the man on it into the waves.

After a long and wearisome hour of work, getting completely drenched, I returned to shelter having done the job; the storm jib was set; casting a last look at it before entering the cabin, I savoured triumph. To tell the truth, once it was over, the task that had looked practically impossible now seemed easy.

Lehg II now sailed better and had lost the tendency to luff; she was easier on the helm.

On the 5th of August a bank of cloud to the South indicated the presence of Tristan da Cunha about 200 miles away. This island is inhabited by a small colony and is only visited once a year, and that for a few hours, by a ship of the Royal Navy; but for me it represented humanity.

Why did I not call there after these thirty-eight days of isolation? For two reasons: currents and winds had carried me far to the north; and, as the island has no port, I could not have rested there. The revictualling ship has to anchor off shore and send in boats. Furthermore, I was in a hurry to get to Africa to have the boat repaired and let my arm heal properly. And I wanted to give some news of myself as soon as possible.

During the days of light breezes I spent most of my time in the cabin; when I came on deck I had the amusement of seeing some little grey petrels doing aerobatics round my rigging.

The current had carried me off course to the North, and if my meridian of the 6th of August was correct, I was 200 miles too high. That should teach me not to rely too much on my dead reckoning in future. The magnetic variation was very considerable: already 28° and increasing.

I was frequently becalmed and carried along by the current. It seemed to me, contrary to what I had been told, that these calms set in after the full moon; the storms we had to endure— we, for both the boat and I suffered in the struggle—appeared to grow with the crescent moon to a simultaneous climax.

On the 10th of August, thanks to heavy squalls from the South, I was able to make 110 miles with a double gain to the South and West. Latitude 34° gave me more wind; and on the 11th I was only 3°45′ W. of Greenwich. Slowly but surely I was nibbling away the first leg of my voyage.

Up to the present I had not seen the slightest sign of human life; so the sight of a bit of floating cork was an event; another one was the discovery of a tropical cockroach, an insect I have always detested and which I was surprised to find on board. Unfortunately I did not succeed in catching it.

Next day at 07.30 I encountered a monster, a grampus over 30 ft. long; and for the first time I saw a numerous flock of birds, a sign that land was nearer, though still over 1,000 miles away.

But what did absolute distance matter, compared with this manifestation of life? I was getting forward, that was all that mattered. A few days more and I would meet people; I would talk
and laugh and, most important of all to me, would have accomplished the first part of my task. As if to confirm the prospect, a
baulk of timber floated by.

On the 13th of August at 02.00 I crossed the meridian of
Greenwich and started to reckon from the East, a thing that had
never happened to me before; I felt like a foreigner here! What
a lot of things would have happened before I got back into W.
longitude: I had still to cross a part of the Atlantic, the immense
and desolate Indian Ocean, a part of the Tasman Sea and a large
slice of the Pacific. Of course, I was not there yet, but all was
going well. This new reckoning of longitude, the signs of human
life, a good lunch well washed down (with lemonade)—what
more could I ask of life? I noted in my log. I had never experienced so great and simple a joy since I had been at sea; so triv-
ial, to tell the truth, since it caused me to write so naïve a sen-
tence and to see the best of life in such details! There was not
much in the way of deeper feelings left in me: to have found
my way back to sea, to have saved the boat, so far: and to have
experienced the miraculous healing of my arm after a fervent
prayer to little St. Teresa of Lisieux.

Yes, all was well; *Lehg II* was sailing much better, took the
waves more smoothly. I had become more accustomed to this
way of life; in the height of the waves I no longer found awe
but amusement: the waves were my friends and I was playing
switchback on them.

Today, the 14th of August, I had beaten my own record of lone
sailing. In 1932 I had taken forty-five days from the Canaries to
the coast of Brazil; this trip so far was one day longer and it gave
me a certain satisfaction, although I did not forget that it was the
shortest leg of my "impossible route."

I had been able to take a series of sights which confirmed the fact that I was nearing the route of ships bound for South Africa. According to my calculation I should arrive on the 22nd; but well before that date I would sight ships. I looked forward to this moment both with joy and anxiety; joy at seeing human beings, anxiety to verify the accuracy of my navigation. I had only one chronometer of which I took the greatest care, winding it each day at the same time, 13.00 hours. Any irregularity would increase my error in longitude. As for latitude, I observed it by sextant with meticulous care. I was quite sure I was making no mistake and certain not to miss that appendage of Africa, the Cape of Good Hope; so sure that I allowed a margin of safety of only 20 miles S. of Cape Town. I could not permit myself an error which, if it proved fatal, would with justice be accounted serious negligence, unpardonable in this region.

Since the last storm the weather had remained reasonable but changeable, demanding perpetual vigilance. I could not rest and allow the boat to sail alone, except when the wind set in the South; so I looked forward with impatience to such moments.

EIGHT

HUMAN VOICES AT LAST

I DO NOT KNOW HOW MANY HOURS I had been asleep. It seemed to be about dawn. I turned over again. But . . . what was that? No, no, impossible! And it was *not* a a dream . . . I heard a siren.

The second blast was longer.

I leapt from my bunk like a jack-in-the-box, banging my head on the panel.

Hurrah! about a hundred metres astern the enormous dark olive hull of a ship making towards me. The deck was crowded with officers and sailors shouting and gesticulating. I motioned them to try to come alongside. Slowly and carefully the ship came abreast of me. Only then did I think of speaking to the crew in English, the language of the sea:

"Captain, my position, please?"

I got a reply, but it was not what I wanted to know. I was so disappointed at not getting the information that I imagined that they had not understood. I collected a speaking-trumpet and put my question again. They only replied with words which did not make sense to me and at all events were not what I wanted: I needed figures, not words.

Interminable, useless seconds passed. I thought of asking them whether they spoke Italian and got a loud "No" in reply. Then I saw the name "*Pyratiny*". . . . I tried in Portuguese and they replied in the same language:

"Why didn't you come out when we blew the siren?"

"Tell me, Captain, do you never sleep?"

"Ah, you were asleep!"

I asked for confirmation of my position but was told that I could not have it. It was wartime . . . they were not allowed to give information.

In the meantime, a member of the crew had recognized me and soon everyone on board knew who I was. It was a Brazilian ship. I asked them to send the following message to the Argentine Minister of Marine when they next touched port: "*Lehg* sailing nothing to report."

Before we parted, I insisted:

"I'm at 34° S. by 6°15′ E., am I not? About 700 miles from the Cape of Good Hope?"

"No," replied the captain, but without conviction, "but carry on as you are. You're on the right course."

"Yes," someone corrected, rather irritably, "provided the wind stays as it is."

More salutes; we parted and she went her way.

From time to time I popped out of the cabin to convince myself that I had not been dreaming. No, there were the masts and funnel, gradually getting smaller. Soon there was only a smudge ahead on the horizon.

I was left with the happy feeling of having spoken and the satisfaction of knowing from several indications that my navigation had been correct.

The night was calm. The moon appeared on the horizon. I looked into the depths, trying to distinguish something. Everything was phosphorescent. Fish were dashing about: some of the bolder ones passed under the keel. A kaleidoscopic world of strange light.

The whole night would not have been enough to appease my curiosity. But the calm would not last, could not last, in these regions. In fact, it was rather abnormal. The barometer, which always knows best, started to fall. And now a violent East wind started blowing in my teeth—a rare phenomenon in this region and exactly what I did not want.

But I was so accustomed to inconveniences that I accepted this curb on my impatience in the same way that I accepted the routine of baling—which I have passed over in silence but which unfortunately was still necessary—and that of the dressings which continued as well. Sometimes an awkward movement would give the damaged limb a knock. But all that was nothing compared to the satisfaction of seeing the boat rising through the masses of spray that tried to smother her.

For the storm prophesied by the barometer was well and truly there. Everything was creaking. I spent long hours at the helm, with all sail set, except that the mainsail was replaced by the storm trysail. The waves were battering *Lehg II*.

In that series of squalls the only hours had for sleep were from 02.00 till daybreak. During that time I lowered the trysail. I lost 30 miles by doing so, but I had to have more rest; every time I had tried to stay more than thirty hours at the helm the result had been bad.

On the 20th I noticed that the mizzen was coming unsewn in some places. The wind, now blowing from the West with furious squalls, did not permit me to mend it, and I had to wait for the early morning lull to do so. Having done the job, I went below; but at three a terrible crash made me feel that *Lehg II* was sinking. I was in my bunk surrounded by bottles, broken glass and tins of food which had been hurled at me. Fortunately none of these projectiles had hit me fair and square; it might have killed me.

The hull was horizontal and a torrent of water was pouring through the hatch; slowly she straightened up. It was easy to guess what had happened: carrying so little canvas the boat had got blanketed under a breaking wave, which laid her on her beam ends.

Everything below was in a horrible mess. Tins of butter were mixed up with needles and thread. Partitions had been torn out; water, swilling to and fro, was wrecking the cabin. I set to work.

By dawn order was more or less restored. On deck the only sign of the accident was that the metal weather-vane from the masthead had been carried away.

I was 210 miles from my first landfall. During the day I saw one ship, but very far away.

During the night of the 22nd of August the weather improved and invited a contemplative mood. At peaceful moments I find that daydreaming is a spiritual need. I watched the flight of clouds, the relics of the gale, as they drifted slowly eastward; I should have liked to go with them to see what awaited me farther on. I wished for the power to amend or avoid so many errors, to be able to direct lost humanity on to the right path, to achieve something beyond normal human capacity. . . . I felt an urge for unity and harmony with the majesty of the starlit night around me; and words were pitifully inadequate, almost an insult to the grandeur there unfolded. I sang an Ave Maria.

Reality brought me tumbling back to earth. I saw to the S.E. two ships without lights and tried to attract their attention with my electric torch. I imagine that they must have taken me for a camouflaged submarine, for their smoke showed that they were crowding on steam in their haste to avoid me. And soon I was alone again on the sea, looking at the stars beyond my mast-head with its missing pennant, the only sign of an incident that might have meant the end of the journey. Perhaps something of me went overboard with that little sheet of metal?

I went below, and before getting into my bunk I knelt down as I did every evening: time for prayers.

When I made the first entries in my log for the 31st of August I certainly had no idea what this day would bring, nor that it would be a milestone, for ever memorable in my life as a sailor.

It was a stormy daybreak; the sun shone fitfully and the sea was getting up under the sou'wester. Between two waves a cachalot whale appeared and vanished rapidly. But astern . . . ? Could I be mistaken? I thought I had a glimpse of a ship. I was more often in the hollow of the waves than on their crest and it was hard to be certain.

But I was not left long in doubt. It was certainly a ship, but she was light, empty. She must have been making over 25 knots in such a sea. What could she be? At times it seemed to me that she was a yacht. She was pitching heavily, appearing and vanishing, but getting rapidly closer. I hoisted Argentine colours and got out my speaking-trumpet. And now she tackled me in Morse with a Scott lamp. I could not reply; I waved my arms to try to make them understand.

The warship, for such she was, came closer. The officers on the bridge asked me my name in English. Now, I had learnt that language, rather badly, at school, and had not spoken it for over twenty years. We had some difficulty in making ourselves understood.

"Where are you bound?"

"The Cape."

"Why?" I was asked rather testily.

"To rest."

"Why in that port?"

"There is no other ahead of me."

"Why choose that one?"

I explained that after doing some 4,000 miles I felt I deserved a rest.

I thought I saw a smile.

At this precise moment I was rather shattered to see something emerging from the waves quite close to me. It was a submarine.

The questions went on. I then asked whether it would not be possible to speak French. One officer volunteered to interpret but soon gave it up, explaining that he had not spoken that language for years. Then a voice, not from the the bridge but from aft, remarked:

"How goes it, old man?" in perfect Spanish.

The first words in my language for fifty-five days! All eyes turned to the stern of the ship, even those of the submarine crew huddled on the conning tower. With these words, which only I had understood—and with what joy!—everyone burst out laughing and gesticulating. The humble sailor, our interpreter, suddenly became important.

No machine gun ever spoke so fast as I. My interlocutor was riddled, harassed, overwhelmed with words. I told him where I came from, who I was, what I was doing or not doing, what I wanted and what I didn't want . . . but suddenly a wave made me lose my balance and deposited me in the cockpit. A gale of laughter arose—I joined in.

The commander asked whether I needed anything. No thanks. When did I expect to make land? That same night.

"Impossible," he replied. "You're still over 50 miles away."

"I shall be in port this very night," I insisted.

They told me the way—I was on the right course, and after friendly greeting drew away. The submarine, surfaced, passed *Lehg II* hull to hull; we were evidently going the same way.

The weather, the heavy seas, the wind, everything looked rosy. I felt happy, full of love and life. I thought of the pride all my Latin American brethren would feel when they heard that the South Atlantic had been conquered.

It was 16.00 hours; flocks of birds were wheeling round me, birds of species that never go far from land; below me the immense swell of that Cape which was once called the Cape of Storms.

On the leaden horizon to the N.E. I seemed to distinguish a patch that was darker than the rest. I looked, I stared, and thought that I could at last identify Table Mountain.

Land. For fifty-five days I had seen none. The miracle had happened. It was true! Before my hungry eyes the mountain was growing, taking shape; thickening clouds came and veiled the summit but not the foot. I took cross-bearings. Already my mind was at rest; I had made landfall and it didn't matter what time I arrived; I was there.

It was a wise precaution to take bearings, for the land was soon obscured and I was not to see it before nightfall.

Lehg II was spanking along.

Something was floating ahead; as I came closer I saw two seals resting on a baulk of wood. At the sight of me they dived.

Dusk was falling; I passed a mine-sweeper manoeuvring and we dipped flags to each other. But the swell was so heavy that we lost sight of each other at times, less than a hundred yards apart. It got dark; there were many bright lights abeam; it looked like Rio de Janeiro bay. Bit by bit I advanced, hearing sounds of traffic while wind and waves grew less.

As I rounded Greenpoint, two searchlights, one from the top of Table Mountain, the other from Robben Island, were focused on me. No doubt to identify me.

A cutter approached in the darkness; someone hailed me:
"Your name?"

I replied; the vessel saluted and went about. Farther in a little tug offered to pilot me. I declined with thanks.

"You can't come in without a pilot," he yelled.

I pointed out that I knew my way and that I was a yacht, not a merchantman. I had not forgotten my little store of £10: a pilot would cost £5, and my capital would be halved.

The pilot went off swearing at me; he could not have sailed very many seas.

In the meantime I was nearing the port; its red light had been visible for the last two hours. The lights of the harbour launch appeared ahead; I could hear the pilot telling how his services had been refused.

"Well, it's a yacht."

"These *verdomde* sailing ships always make us lose money," he grumbled into the darkness.

The crew of the harbour launch welcomed me and came with me into the port, where I made fast alongside an enormous vessel undergoing repairs. The crew leapt aboard and helped me to lower the mainsail: the staysail had been set for fifty-five days.

I did not feel tired at all. It was 22.00 hours. In a few moments I was boarded by a whole series of official craft; the Harbour Master, the Customs, the police and the camaraderie that unites all sailors in the world took over at once.

Half an hour later I felt that I was dreaming. On board of a motionless *Lehg II* more than ten persons were celebrating her success in rum that had crossed the Atlantic. The bottles passed from mouth to mouth; we drank and drank again. With the stub of the last cigarette of three packets smoked without stopping, I lit a South African cigarette that was passed to me.

At three in the morning these new friends departed; I remained alone and disposed myself to enjoy my rest.

It was far from perfect.

Many nights were to pass before I stopped rushing up on deck with my heart in my mouth, to make sure that I really was in port.

NINE

START AGAIN

THE NEXT MORNING saw the procession of journalists and photographers. They were all full of congratulations.

With several friends from the British Navy I went ashore. My legs felt very odd—was it an earthquake? No; *Lehg II* who, I could hardly realize it, had crossed this incredible stretch of sea, my darling *Lehg II* was swaying peacefully at her moorings in the calm water of the harbour.

We called at the Harbour Master's office and an officer began to explain how to bring my documents up to date. But his chief interrupted, pushing a pass in front of him.

"This is for Mr. Dumas. He can come and go as he pleases."

I was taken to the officers' mess and went to have a wash: one handed me a towel, another a comb, a third lit my cigarette. They waited on me hand and foot. The Garrison Commander and the S.N.O. were there; a special cocktail was mixed in my honour. The S.N.O. had read the book of my first voyage.[†]

Lunch followed. I was being overwhelmed with kindness without being able to express my gratitude properly.

I was called to the telephone. The telephone? For me? Who in this country can be ringing me up? I was afraid of being unable to cope with a telephone conversation in English, but it was the Argentine Consul, who soon joined us.

At the end of the meal I noticed for the first time that people

---

[†]"Solo Rumbo a la Cruz del Sur."

were staring at me with curiosity. My God! I had driven in a car, been about in the town, met all the V.I.P.s, had lunch in a first-class restaurant . . . dressed in tattered old trousers, a pullover with the elbows out, a handkerchief round my neck and no hair-cut. The next day's papers described me as being "picturesquely dressed, with the air of a filibuster."

I had made a hard-and-fast plan: to stay twenty days at the Cape and not do anything about the boat until the last week. I wanted to put work on one side completely for a while. I was able to moor *Lehg II* in a quiet spot near the quay and spent the first few days looking round.

Cape Town lies in practically the same latitude as Buenos Aires and Montevideo, and the climate is excellent except when the East wind stirs up coal dust in the port area. It is a modern city with a very important port and a network of magnificent roads leading to practically all parts of the Union of South Africa and running through varied landscapes of surprising beauty.

My South American eyes were caught particularly by the trolleybuses in the central part of the town; practically all double-deckers with women as conductors. Another characteristic detail was the helmets worn by the police, as in London.

The segregation between white and coloured is very marked, to the point where teashops display a notice "Reserved for Euro-

peans." The buses and cinemas for the whites may not be used by coloured people, who have their own.

A bar, run by an Englishman who talked only with one side of his mouth and smiled only with half his face (probably so that the other half should not know), displayed the same sign. But . . . the most curious circumstance is that adjoining this bar was another, identical in form and decoration, communicating with the first by a door situated behind the barman. One place was for whites, the other for blacks. Two halves of bar, two halves of expression . . .

I was never able to determine which side caught the barman's smile and which his straight face.

TEN

. . . AND CARRY ON

FROM THE WORLD I had left behind me came news: telegrams from Buenos Aires and Montevideo. They were joined by letters of congratulation from South Africa.

I was particularly struck by one of these; it was obviously written by a cultured woman.

She belonged to a seafaring family from Holland and showed her enthusiasm for everything connected with the sea. She lived with her family in a villa nestling close to the sea in a quiet little spot, and asked me to call.

On a sunny afternoon I decided to go and make her acquaintance. The spot—Camps Bay—and the villa made a perfect picture, a little world of its own. Quite close by, the tired Atlantic swell rolled in to die, gently, on the beach. A spot one would like to come back to.

I was received by a fair-haired young woman, some 30 years of age, who was fond enough of nature to go swimming even in winter. She had taken this house in exchange for a finer one on the hillside which she had previously owned, to be nearer the sound of the sea which had an irresistible ancestral appeal to her. She had dreams of living in the Seychelles, near the Equator in the Indian Ocean; she knew them well and spoke with enthusiasm of their beauty and their pleasant climate.

The company of a person with such a taste for beauty and so much understanding of the things that meant much to me was most agreeable; and this house was a refuge for me in days of uncertainty.

My new friend spoke several languages and possessed a very comprehensive background of travel and culture. One day she said:

"Why go on with your voyage?"

Would I not like to settle there?

What she could not understand was that my placidity was that of a calm at sea; it would not last. And whilst reason and inclination urged me to stay, I looked for a way of breaking the spell.

I could neither promise to stay nor say that I was going.

I remembered the proverb: "Never let your friend's hand get hot in yours." This calm sea, this lovely spot, this mildness, was balm to me; it mingled with the picture of that island in the Indian Ocean, a dream rather than anything earthly. Why go on with the voyage? Because . . . because nothing else would do; because there remained in my hand a little of the warmth of other hands, that warmth that strikes deeper and deeper till it reaches the heart. I confessed to myself that one day I should say "*à demain*" and that tomorrow would never come.

One evening I was trying to describe our pampa and reading passages of "Martin Fierro," haltingly translated to illustrate my meaning: I was sitting under the light of a single lamp, which left the rest of the room in semi-darkness. I lifted my eyes to rest for a moment.

Outside, the moonlight on the sea made a track to the West, as if to show me where my home lay. A path of light. . . . A sign, but I hardly knew what it meant at that moment. There was the West, that was where I had to go. And if I did not get there I would get nowhere. Neither the harmony of the South African night on the white beach, nor the generous hospitality, like calm waters where my spirit could rest—nothing could hold me. I had sailed from Buenos Aires into the rising sun; now the moon seemed to be showing me this point of departure and demanding my return. The moment had come. I said "*à demain;*" it was "goodbye."

I have kept two letters, the prologue and the epilogue of this moment of my life. The first is the invitation; the second says:

"Lord Byron affirmed that in the course of his life he had only known three hours of happiness. I have had many more: I am happier than he was. I savoured them consciously and lost nothing of them. I understood that the hours you were giving me would destroy in a few moments all those—and they were not many—that I had known before. But I felt that it was better so; and for you I ask only the greatest happiness of all, which is the pursuit of your ideal."

ELEVEN

BUENAS TARDES, SEÑOR!

ON ONE OF THE LAST AFTERNOONS of my stay at the Cape, I visited my friends of the Argentine ship *Menendez* which was about to sail. I was overwhelmed with congratulations and good wishes and they promised to testify to my good morale when they arrived at Buenos Aires; furthermore the captain gave me some canvas to repair my sails and various bits of ironmongery that might come in useful.

As I was going back to *Lehg II*'s berth, not far away, with my parcel under my arm, I heard a voice which said in good Castilian:

"Buenas tardes, Señor!"

I stared at the speaker, for I thought I already knew everyone in the town who spoke Spanish; he must be a South African.

"May I come with you?" he continued.

"With pleasure! Just let me put this parcel aboard, and we'll go somewhere."

And so it was. We started back through the security areas of the port, barred to the general public but for which he, being a ship's chandler, held a permit. I then learnt that he had spent thirty years in Patagonia. He spoke with deep feeling and enthusiasm of the time he had spent in the Argentine and asked me to have a cognac.

We entered one of the numerous bars; friends arrived and the cognac soon multiplied itself by eight, and all the languages of the world were exploding round us like a basket of fireworks.

52

One wore a fez, another a white turban, this one a wide sombrero, the next a cap. The atmosphere was very rich and colourful; it was like a congress of survivors from assorted shipwrecks.

Alcohol spontaneously generates good fellowship, especially in the presence of memories in common. And my companion insisted on taking me home with him to Bella Vista in the suburbs. The train we had to take ran through the cemetery, where there are no fewer than three stops. It is said to be the largest graveyard in the world.

We came to a pleasant house.

"Before we start," said he, "I want to show you something that will shake you no little."

From a drawer of his desk he produced twelve Argentine passports.

"My sons," he said proudly.

Presently the owners of these documents arrived, twelve magnificent young men born in Patagonia. Thanks to one of them, I heard something that I had missed for a very long time, tangoes played on the victrola. A strange sensation—a ghost from the past which one wants to smother and cherish at the same time, which gives pain rather than pleasure. In far-off ports I generally try to get outside myself—outside my memories and my feelings; and that is why I try to interest myself in other people's problems. I therefore listened with great attention when the lady of the house told me of her thirty years in Argentina. She went there young, to seek fortune; she came back home with twelve sons, her only achievement and the only rewards of a long and arduous life.

TWELVE

WASHING UP

IT WAS MIDDAY. Tomorrow I was to go back the sea.

The sun shone out of a leaden sky. I was washing crockery in the cabin.

Lehg II was moored to a little wooden pier belonging to the Lowus company; its proprietor had given me some waterproof paint, which I needed very badly, in exchange for a bottle of whisky.

The damage forward had been so perfectly repaired that no trouble was to be anticipated. Two fishermen had served my shrouds with sheepskin so that the sails should not get stained with rust.

All this cost me £7 and the necessary charts were another £10 and I had £2 left.

The prospects of the "impossible route" across the Indian Ocean were not at all encouraging. The distance was 7,400 miles; and from what I had been able to gather, there was little hope of overcoming so many difficulties. The numerous records of voyages with a tragic end in this zone gave me no rosy outlook for the future.

The Pilot Chart, that precious and indispensable compendium for the navigator, which I carried on every voyage, gives for September–December a probable mean of twenty-seven days per month of winds Force 8 (37–44 knots). And it was precisely in those months that I was to attempt the crossing of the whole breadth of the Indian Ocean.

Lehg II is given a good send-off at Cape Town.

Lehg II starting from Cape Town Harbour at the beginning of
her passage through the Indian Ocean.

But this was not all. To these twenty-seven days of gales per month must be added the risk of cyclones in the region between 100° and 175° E., which includes the Tasman Sea by New Zealand. In these cyclones the wind force rarely falls below 60 knots (Force 11); and through that zone I must pass. This picture should convey what one means by "living to keep watch and keep the sails in repair."

In consequence of the relatively shallow water above the submarine plateau, these winds whip up the sea and create breaking waves which may exceed 40 feet or even 50 feet in height. In the immensity and solitude of this ocean, the second leg of my voyage, I would not encounter any place to put in nor any shelter. On my route lay only two islets, St. Paul and Amsterdam Islands. In case of dire necessity I could indeed take refuge there: on the N. side of the crater of St. Paul there is a store of food and clothing for the shipwrecked; and similar facilities at Amsterdam. But these islands are inhabited only by sea birds, have no beaches on which to land, and above all, one would have to be very lucky to get there.

In this zone the magnetic variation is considerable and magnetic storms severe, the variation reaching 54° W., which necessitates steering a course of 144° by the compass in order to sail due E. This variation changes very rapidly, so that I should have to calculate my route carefully every two or three days, at the same time making a correction for drift to leeward, under penalty of prolonging still further this interminable and wearisome stage.

It was an almost impossible enterprise, but in spite of everything I kept smiling.

What a difference between this trip and a crossing in the region of trade winds, where the boat is quietly, gently wafted across a warm sea; where life flows by in tropical somnolence with marine fauna for company and entertainment during the long hours of watchkeeping, and the journey soon ends in some happy island covered with coconut palms and bordered with beaches of coral sand. And then—to live for the day, far from conventions and civilization so-called, from ready-made ideas, taxation, and especially from the clash of personalities so painful to the sensitive. Lucky are those strong enough to break loose from habit and escape the dreariness of dying on their feet or existing as "zombies." But how many reach the end of their life without ever having lived! Not only to embark on the endless tracks of the sea, but to follow the road of everyday life in simplicity.

Thus I meditated sombrely on the eve of my departure, face to face with the monstrous reality written on the next page of my dance programme—the *valse triste* of this 7,400 mile stage eastward, a sequence of bitter unsmiling tomorrows—unable to define clearly why it was my choice. Tomorrow I should set out on the inhospitable road that no lone navigator had ever followed. When I went to buy charts the old skipper in charge of them said:

"I knew that you were bound to roll up here. Alain Gerbault came to see me. Like everyone else who has sailed a bit, he had a project, a reason for going to sea again some day. He said to me: 'Do you know that there is an almost unkown little island in the Indian Ocean, covered with seals. Work it out; at £5 a pelt we'll be rich. . . .' We'll go there after the war; will that suit you?"

So I went on washing crocks on board *Lehg II*. I looked through the porthole. On the quay several weary-looking negroes, waiting to be hired, were chatting. One of them was humming a weird tune.

I heard the sound of engines and turned round to see a launch enter the port and manoeuvre to lay alongside the quay. I noticed that her ensign was at half-mast; there must be dead aboard. Some marines were standing on deck with flowers in their hands.

When she had made fast, a lorry arrived and stretchers were brought ashore; bodies were swaying under the blankets. *C'est la guerre.*

Monday 14 September.

Lehg II was waiting. With my fellow countryman Glessmann, I went to the grocer's. There was such a lot to take. But there were serious obstacles: rationing and my £2. All that I could buy barely filled a carrier bag. Of course I had basic rations aboard; but I saw many things in the shop that would be very welcome on a run of over 7,000 miles! I had to content myself with some preserves and cheese; and when my friend offered to pay I did not refuse. . . .

Once more the hour of parting was about to strike; the minutes were running out. Quickly I set all sail, pausing to greet the Portuguese and Spanish Consuls as well as the representative of the Royal Cape Yacht Club, most of whose members were serving. Other friends were looking on and drinking in every detail. The Argentine Consul coiled down a rope, no doubt in memory of his sailings on the River Plate. Embraces, handshakes, goodbyes that stuck in the throat, and at 13.00 *Lehg II* started off slowly from the berth where she had remained for twenty days.

Workmen stopped work for a moment to wave to me, some climbing to the bridge, others lined up on deck. I was going so slowly as to get a panoramic view of this section of the port. Between the sheds I could see the masts of that famous sailing vessel the *Pamir*. As I neared the pier in the afternoon sun, a group of friends rushed to the pierhead, and Bill Amman, an enthusiastic yachtsman, could not restrain a cry of admiration.

"How fine she looks with all sail set!"

It was quite true, she was lovely. I looked at her with a certain pride myself.

I was about to pass the pier when a British warship came in. As she passed I saluted her ensign; on his bridge the commander stood to attention and saluted me with a fatherly smile.

From land came cries of "Cheerio, cheerio, cheerio!," the farewells and good wishes of my friends, the stevedores, sailors and what have you.

To get out from under the lee of the land, to catch the wind and get searoom before starting on the high seas, I tacked. This brought me close to a fine American six-master, with a name that thrilled me: it was *Tango*. Some of the crew who had been lying on deck got up as I approached.

"Where are you bound?" they asked.

"For New Zealand."

"Good luck!"

They could imagine what was in store for me. They added:

"The weather's just right for you."

(They say that because they long to put to sea themselves; they had been anchored there for several months.)

Penguins and seals were playing round my boat. At 17.00 hours the fine houses of Green Point were abeam. A patrol vessel dashed up, saluted and went off again. The breeze was light and veering to the S.W. As night drew on it got lighter until I was practically becalmed.

Outward bound ships passed me at speed and I took pleasure in contemplating the lights ashore.

As the moon set I raised a little breeze that helped me on. Near me I heard a seal breathing. I tried to go up into the wind to be clear of all obstacles, but I had to struggle against a strong current.

The next day I got to the level of Duyker Point, but was becalmed in the Atlantic current that switches to the North along the African coast and could make no headway; in twenty-four hours I had only progressed some 10 miles.

In the afternoon a deceptive breeze gave me a slender hope that I might round the Cape of Good Hope, only some 20 miles away, by midnight. But after passing Hout Bay I was becalmed in front of Slang Kop lighthouse; this obliged me to spend the night on deck because of the traffic. Enormous masses of steel hurtled by without lights, only the sound of the engines announcing their coming.

From the coast I could hear the singing of birds mingling with the other noises of the immense African continent. Shore lights were twinkling under a blaze of stars. This was a generous compensation for my solitude. The dream-like spectacle left me in a kind of trance. *Lehg II* was barely leaving a phosphorescent wake.

On the 16th of September the sunrise was very pale. After fifty hours' calm the wind set in the north. *Lehg II* began to get headway, and I tried to make up for lost time. Hout, Chapman's Peak and Slang Kop were left behind. On my port bow a high promontory jutted into the sea; the Cape of Good Hope, discovered by Vasco da Gama in 1497 on his way to India. This "cape of storms" was for a long time an unavoidable passage for all the ships of the world.

On this sunless morning its silhouette stuck out harsh and jagged against the sky, cold lines on a cold morning.

Excitement grew as I approached it. The swell was getting up; as it came from astern it helped the wind to carry me on. The cape was now abeam, but I had to continue steering South for half a mile in order to clear two rocks that mount guard seaward. I took a bearing and when I was sure of being clear of danger I tacked due East.

Soon a line of wind-torn breakers showed that I had passed the rocks. The historic moment had come: it was 10.00 hours on the 16th and I had rounded the Cape of Good Hope. Thus the Atlantic crossing was truly finished and I set forth on the impossible journey across the Indian Ocean. Up to the present no one had ventured alone into the regions I was about to cross.

THIRTEEN

THE WORST OF ALL

I HAD EXPERIENCED HARDSHIP in the Atlantic, and perhaps that gave me confidence for the future; but the reality, the frightening reality of what lay before me, was to surpass anything that I had experienced before in my life as a sailor. It was more painful and more terrifying than the short passage through the Bay of Biscay on my 1932 cruise.

With all sail set and a fair wind the boat was running at full speed. The swell was irregular and got heavier as I passed Rocky Bank. Two patrol vessels, put out from False Bay, sailed towards me, but they soon gave up the attempt on account of the gigantic swell and returned to the shelter of the land.

In front lay Hangklip Point; farther on Danau, the detached end of a mountain range, jutted out into the sea.

In accordance with my programme I tried by every measure to hug the coast as close as possible, so that when I came to Needle Point the current off the reef, which reaches 4 knots (100 miles in twenty-four hours), should not carry me too far South. The swell was much stronger there; it was already very noticeable here, in a depth of 30 fathoms.

Night fell and I could not leave the tiller for a moment. I was driving with all sail set, without lights, through the inky night and the storm. The glass was falling; the gale had not yet reached its climax. If there was to be any change it would certainly not be for the better. Every sign indicated that I had the worst to fear; I had no confidence whatever.

Out of the trough of the waves dead ahead emerged the dim outline of a ship on the opposite course. She was, of course, without lights and pitching badly. She was making heavy weather, for she was head on to the seas.

Gradually she disappeared astern.

On the horizon to windward, flashes of light from the Needles lighthouse cut through the darkness. As I drew near I got the feeling of blows struck into the empty air, beams that tried in vain to pierce the darkness. This is an occulting light with three eclipses; at times the rays of light seemed like sentient beings, struggling desperately to survive this black night.

I was getting on well to the East. At midnight the wind suddenly dropped, and before I could note what was going on a squall from the South struck me. With it came low cloud; and soon the flashes from the lighthouse disappeared in the murk. Visibility was very bad and I feared that, with this change of conditions, the wind might pick me up and cast me ashore in Struys Bay.

I set about shortening sail in order to get into the wind and so away from the coast.

I had not slept for many hours, to all intents and purposes since I left port.

On the 17th at 03.00 hours I could no longer keep awake; I decided to sleep in spite of the weather and lowered the mainsail. And so I let her sail on alone, waking every now and then to see what was happening.

At daybreak I was able to return to the helm and to check my course properly. I saw an enormous whale. I had sailed 143 miles in twenty-four hours.

In the afternoon I heard the drone of an aircraft and saw a bomber flitting through the clouds. No doubt a patrol; he flew over me and went his way.

Land had disappeared; I was not to see it again for several months.

FOURTEEN

LEGENDS OF THE SEA

ON THE NIGHT of the 19th of September I was sailing in the region where the ghost of the phantom ship has been seen.

She was known as the *Flying Dutchman*. The captain is said to have been seen on stormy nights driving his crew to pile on sail in order to round the Cape of Good Hope.

All sailors tell these stories; and things are actually experienced at sea that seem fantastic to landsmen.

Take for example the case of the brig *Mary-Céleste*, found on the high sea with all sail set and no trace of a human being aboard. The table was properly set and a meal was ready in the galley; everything was in order. This mystery has never been satisfactorily solved.

Another story which I can now tell (for at the time I should have been taken for a lunatic) happened to me ten years ago.

I was two days from Arcachon when one night, off Bilbao, the silence of the sea was broken by a conversation which I heard distinctly; it was almost monosyllabic.

Two people appeared to be speaking.

I was astounded. I asked myself how they could have come aboard, for I had not left the boat for twenty-four hours previous to sailing.

They could only be hidden forward in a locker that I never used, with a small door which separated it completely from the rest of *Lehg I.*

"Listen," said a voice with a strong Spanish accent, "I'm going to look for something to eat."

"Shut up; he'll hear you."

"No, he won't."

It was nearly 30 feet from the tiller to that point, which was also hidden by the mast; the fore hatch might well have been open.

At the moment I did not dare to speak, but I sought for a logical explanation of the presence of these individuals.

One of them frequently asked for cigarettes. I also heard a number of unusual sounds which satisfied me that there were strangers aboard.

Twenty-four hours went by; the storm which had blown up did not permit me to leave the helm. My own struggle for life, if it did not make me forget what was going on, at least inspired me with pity for my stowaways; as it was practically impossible to hang on aft, I could imagine what it was like for them forward. I resolved to hail them as soon as the storm had blown over and put them ashore at some port or other.

The wind lasted three days and three nights. Three feet of water was playing hell below.

On the night I was nearing Ferrol, having rounded Cape Ortegal, I called out to them to come forth from their hiding-place. No one answered. I went on, explaining that I understood; I went below and, armed with a gaff, searched every cranny where they might have hidden. I struck matches; I found nothing.

Returning to the helm, very puzzled, I could see no other solution to the mystery than that they had tried to swim ashore.

After this happened to me, nothing could surprise me any longer. What can arise out of the depths of the sea? Who knows what lies beyond this life? Who can sound the unknown? Our poor senses are feeble instruments.

There is St. Elmo's fire, seen by many sailors, which

announces a storm. And I have myself heard many voices at sea accompanied by the sound of bells. There is a state of mind, peculiar to the sailor, which is simple and human because it does not deal in subtleties. Alone at sea and near to God, who can know whether the environment is not in tune with strange forces?

On the stormy night when I recalled these memories I was sailing in the area where legend—unless it be reality—places the appearances of the phantom ship. They are actually recorded on one of my charts.

The new day dawned reluctantly. My boat was running with all sail set in a stormy sea; my position was 36°10′ S. by 24°45′ E. The patrolling aircraft went by, as it did every morning. That day I managed to salute the crew by waving my arm.

I had not been entirely successful in overcoming the current that was carrying me towards the South.

I escaped from the helm for a few moments to see whether *Lehg II* had made much water in the last twenty-four hours. Alas! I was distressed to find that the bilge was full; I could not understand it till I discovered that it was fresh water. The hammering we had undergone had started the rivets of the forward tank, which held 40 gallons. A rapid calculation showed that all I had left was a 20 gallon tank, a 2 gallon demijohn and a 10 gallon breaker. I should have to make do with that.

I went back to keep watch and saw that the wind had dropped. The clouds were very low and I was frightened to see three waterspouts approaching from the North. The clouds were whirling as if boiling in a gigantic kettle. I reckoned the diameter of each spout at 300 yards; they were spinning furiously and sucking up water. It is not known with certainty whether these spouts go right up to the cloud mass. The spectacle, terrifying as it is, has a certain grandiose beauty.

They were bearing down on me rapidly. I tacked in order to

avoid them, but there was so little wind that this manoeuvre went slowly. Seconds and minutes passed in trepidation; but fortunately the spouts went by at a distance of some 500 yards. My breathing returned to normal; the skirts of death had brushed me.

It is said that an American warship went deliberately through the centre of a waterspout so that her captain could assess the possible damage; it seems that, apart from two smashed lifeboats, the superstructure suffered only minor damage. But it must not be forgotten that the ship was protected by her length. *Lehg II* was only 9 metres 55 long, and if the spout had caught her she would have whirled like the sea-water. I prefer not to think of the result.

I tried to organize for the best in the circumstances, but perfection was unattainable because the situation kept changing. I stayed at the helm as long as possible in order to reach New Zealand before the cyclone season. My daily runs were 120 to 150 miles (an average of 5 to 6 knots), which was excellent. In order to achieve this I had to crowd on all canvas—on this infernal ocean—whilst I was at the helm. The waves were breaking on the whole surface of the sea. I could not avoid those that broke on the deck, drenching me completely and wrecking my outer clothing.

In the cabin the temperature remained about 15°C., but on the deck the cold struck through the Balaclava cap on my head.

I was wearing several pullovers under my oilskin, but the latter was in such a state that it was no longer any protection.

The wind stayed in the West. Weather permitting, usually at dawn, I made myself a large cup of chocolate, accompanied by dates and sea biscuit well buttered. This rather odd diet, supplemented with bar chocolate, kept me in excellent physical condition. I was strong and in perfect health and did not appear to be losing weight. I corrected the diet by adding vitamins A and

C to take the place of fresh food and keep scurvy at bay. Before leaving Buenos Aires I had been examined by five doctors, who affirmed that I had nothing to worry about: man and boat were both seaworthy.

For several days I had not seen an aircraft nor indeed any sign of human life.

One day I remembered that it was my forty-second birthday and decided to celebrate. I prepared a feast; to begin with, the inevitable chocolate for breakfast. Then in the evening, a delicious soup of vegetable meal, jam, sweets and other delicacies, washed down with champagne.

I was running against a strong current which worked up the sea. I hoped that as I gained longitude it would be less strong and the sea less choppy.

The spells of bad weather in the part of the Atlantic I had left in my wake and in this part of the Indian Ocean had nothing in common with those of the Bay of Biscay. The mean depth of those oceans is over 2,000 fathoms and no continent is near enough to break the full force of the wind; the latter raises waves with a trough up to 50 to 60 ft. deep and 900 to 1,200 ft. from crest to crest, and in the South Atlantic there is always a ground swell.

The Pilot Chart had been my Bible, but reality surpassed everything I had been told. And if, by careful steering, I had managed up to the present to defend myself against the massive avalanches of water which this chaos unleashes, it was due in some degree to the shortness of my boat, her rig, and the shape of her hull. I do not think I exaggerate when I say that *no* ship, whether under sail or mechanically propelled, can navigate without risk in these latitudes.

Not so far to the North lay Madagascar; farther on, Réunion and Mauritius; still farther away, Rodriguez Island; all ports of call that I must eschew in order to follow my route as planned.

There was indeed nothing to prevent me from varying my route to stop there, have a rest and learn some history, but I was riding the seas to demonstrate a possibility, and I stuck to it.

For the first time on this run *Lehg II* was sailing alone under full sail. Squalls came in regular succession, all laden with rain. It was interesting to note that with every one the barometer fell 3 mm.

Fortunately I adapted myself to circumstances and got into the habit of taking this sea and these conditions for granted. Up to the present, life rolled by without any remarkable incident: nevertheless, in the depth of my consciousness was a latent, unsurmountable feeling of apprehension that kept me on the alert. I was very conscientious with my navigation; I watched the barometer, thermometer and hygrometer and took sights whenever possible. This work, which the state of the sea rendered rather tricky, gave me great joy, as I could mark the tiny gain on my chart; each day a little step forward a little dot beyond the last.

On the 28th of September I was 1,100 miles out from Cape Town: in fourteen days, allowing for the initial calms, I had made satisfactory progress.

I had no time to be bored. I have often been asked how I filled in the day in the course of my long cruises; people cannot conceive the idea of life without cinemas, theatres and especially human society.

It is said that solitude is best shared with another. These seas offer joys to anyone who is capable of loving and understanding nature. Are there not people who can spend hours watching the rain as it falls? I once read somewhere that three things could never be boring: passing clouds, dancing flames and running water. They are not the only ones. I should add in the first place, work. The self-sufficient man acquires a peculiar state of mind which may be reflected in these pages.

At nightfall on the 28th big black clouds invaded the sky; as I had been struggling ceaselessly against violent winds and a sea that allowed me no rest, I now decided to set a course that would take the boat, sailing on her own, gradually to the North, where better weather might be expected. The length of my runs therefore began to diminish. On the 29th I made only 93 miles and 114 on the following day.

The wind set in the North, which allowed *Lehg II* to sail unattended. As I drew away from high latitudes (in relation to the hemisphere) the sun showed itself more frequently and the temperature rose to 20°C.

Although the mean depth of the Indian Ocean is 2,500 fathoms, its colour is a lighter blue than that of the Atlantic. I was sailing along the northern limit of drift ice. I was not specially concerned with ice, although it may have been the cause of many unexplained shipwrecks. The counter-current which traverses the Indian Ocean from West to East helped me along.

The hours of my first day in this part of the ocean passed more slowly. Sky and water. A few Cape pigeons and the inevitable albatross kept me company.

On the 1st of October I made 113 miles, the following day 100. Numerous porpoises played round me. Their presence was probably due to the proximity of the Crozet Islands, discovered by Mallon du Fresne in 1772; they were only 610 miles away. One of them, Hog Island, contains a store of provisions for castaways.

On the 3rd, thanks to the wind, which after backing from N. to W. had set in the S.W., I made 113 miles and sailed even deeper into the region of low cloud with which I was to become well acquainted.

On my first day in those parts wind and sea dropped; I took advantage of this to cook some mashed potatoes and pillao rice—a consolation for the rough days when it was impossible to cook at all. Cooking is not an unpleasant task, it is even a relaxation from an interminable day at the helm.

And so began a series of identical days in light breezes; my daily runs dwindled to 67 miles, then to 40 miles, and this thanks to the current alone. I was in fact well into what the English call "horse latitudes," where the winds rise above the clouds leaving them motionless. Then the current itself grew slack and I saw no more albatrosses; these birds need a wind. Only porpoises appeared from time to time. That very impressive ocean had become as calm as a lake.

I solaced monotony by imaginary journeys to places like Colombo, Ceylon, Bombay, ancient India, Calcutta, Rangoon—lands of legend, some of them discovered by Vasco da Gama in 1498, others described by Marco Polo, which I hope some day to visit. They were many miles away, but the Réunion group was only 780 miles from my position on the 5th of October.

On the 7th I was amused by an albatross riding on the sea. He was very interested in the activities of a big dorado (*coryphæna*) which was hunting small fish. All this was going on very near him, but outside the reach of his beak, with which he pecked the water at intervals as if to claim a stake in the game. The dorado was making great leaps out of the water in his pursuit. But *Lehg II* drifted slowly away on the current and I never knew who won.

Tiny fish were swimming round the boat. In the night a massive dark bulk passed me, going northwards; a whale, no doubt; the heavy rhythm of his breathing broke the silence of the night. Later on an enormous fish leapt near the bows.

In the afternoon of the 11th I took advantage of a light breeze from the West which soon veered to the N.W., to set a southerly course and get out of this calm.

The zone of the "horse latitudes" is easily recognized: on their southern edge one can see the high clouds driven by the roaring forties, those terrible winds which I certainly had to cultivate if I were to make any progress.

The roving eye looks out for something new; everything is interesting. Among the clouds of all shapes and colours I picked out two that seemed to give the figure 99. What did it mean? Perhaps the duration of my second leg, to New Zealand. It turned out to be very near the truth (104 days).

Then my attention was drawn to a committee of albatrosses. Ten of them in a circle, their beaks directed to a central point which they were examining with interest. As I got nearer, I saw that the object under discussion was a small jar. They sounded rather like ducks, but with a deeper pitch, and seemed to be holding a conference on the origin of this inedible object.

I was getting on; I had reached 35° S. by 64°45′ E.; course E. a quarter S.E. The seas were getting heavier and I had to put on my oilskins. The wind was changeable, never staying more than twenty-four hours in the same quarter. The temperature in the cabin fell to 15°C. I was nearing the islands of Amsterdam and St. Paul, which were over 500 miles to the east, but which seemed nearer on my wind chart. The wind freshened in the East; the barometer, already at 773, was still rising.

As I had finished my first tin of biscuits, I set about opening the second with a hammer and chisel—unaccustomed labour and so a welcome change. When I had unsoldered the lid a piece of wrapping paper appeared. On it was written: "I wish you a pleasant journey; your friend Innocencio, 22 June 1942." Buenos Aires was so far; and in the course of past months I had had so few occasions to refresh my memories of the town I had left, that I felt deeply moved.

Everything round me was so familiar! The things under my eyes were silent witnesses of past struggles, the intimate universe of the seaman; my sail-mending kit was thirty years old, the tobacco box in which I kept my matches, and the pricker for the Primus, had crossed the Bay of Biscay and the Atlantic with me; the ashtray, an empty sardine tin, was an old friend. Indeed wherever I looked I saw some tried and trusted companion. And now a stranger pops up unexpectedly out of the box: a few lines. . . .

To keep matters under control I seized a swab and set about the floorboards; I did not want any witnesses, silent though they were, to my weakness.

The boat was taking a hammering; a big wave broke over the deck from starboard; we shipped a good deal of sea, the cockpit was awash and the water slopped over the zinc coaming into the bottom. More unwelcome work. I did it and returned to the helm; it was very heavy weather and raining hard. The rain was pouring down the mizzen and splashing on my oilskin; sometimes the squalls caught it and dashed it in my face, though I tried to protect myself with a piece of canvas worn as a sou'wester.

Visibility was diminishing; at times I could not see the waves ahead of *Lehg II* as she worked her way to the Southeast. I had run out of this region to find calmer weather, but peace and quiet had palled. Here there was life and movement and, although not a pleasant spot, it was the best for making progress.

The drops falling on my knees formed a pond; to keep the water from running through to my already wet clothes I brushed it off with the canvas of the binnacle housing in a mechanical gesture.

The hull surged and fell again into the trough of the waves. I looked ahead. Nothing in sight but the dark plain of the sea, ridged with white-caps. The lowering sky was like a prison wall. Nothingness—but I was used to it; I threw a cigarette stub overboard and hummed a tune.

Early on the 24th of October I passed Amsterdam Island with its volcanic peaks rising to over 1,000 metres. St. Paul lies quite near it to the North. I had no intention of stopping and in fact I did not see the islands, only a bank of clouds that marks these insignificant and desert spots in the Indian Ocean. All I could possibly find there would be some shipwrecked mariner waiting for death.

The storm did not slacken and the shallower soundings made the sea choppy. Several times when going aft I could not avoid being drenched by a wave. As the days went by I struck deeper into the roaring latitudes and noticed that albatrosses were becoming more numerous.

There is no doubt that these birds are the kings of sail. Their gliding is superb, their weight and power giving them a masterly control over flight.

A smaller bird, the stormy petrel, has a most curious flight, designed perhaps to attract the fish on which it feeds: it flies very rapidly in circles or in zig-zags falling from one wing to the other; then, as if dizzy, it skims the water and with the help of its little feet it dashes up a wave as one going upstairs in a hurry. It carries on with this exercise indefatigably, all day long; and I never saw one settle. It is quite small. I do not know how it can come so far from land unless, being so small, it sometimes settled in this immensity without my noticing it.

Lehg II was sailing in a roaring, majestic inferno. The waves exceeded 40 to 50 feet, stood up like walls and rushed along at a great speed. When I was in the trough I could hardly believe that the boat would rise again instead of going to the bottom in 1,500 fathoms. I saw some seaweed floating. The magnetic variation was almost 35° W. I was still more than 1,800 miles from Australia, forty days out from Cape Town.

The cold was intense.

My linen was in a sorry state. Try as I might, I could not allow *Lehg II* to sail alone except for a few hours at night; sailing as she was with a following wind, she occasionally luffed, but this had little effect on the daily run; so I could get some rest and bale the water that was still seeping through some crack in the deck.

I ate what I had; I mixed cockles or peas with rice. As I was constantly drenched, caloric deficiency was making itself felt, and in the evening I found it necessary to drink rum or brandy; I took it down like water.

FIFTEEN

MY FRIEND THE PIGEON

A NEW KIND OF PORPOISE had appeared. They had white bellies and tails and light brown backs. I saw numerous petrels, little birds with an easy flight which are supposed to announce storms. My daily runs varied from 93 to 103 miles; the temperature in the cabin had fallen to 12°C.

I often amused myself by throwing scraps of biscuit to the birds, who flung themselves upon it. One Cape pigeon stayed by me for nearly the whole of my crossing of the Indian Ocean. He used to arrive and fly round the boat every day and then disappear. Quite one of the family; he would fly ahead of the boat and alight, as though expecting scraps of biscuit as I passed. When the albatrosses came, they would drive him off and I would not see him until the next day, when he came regularly to be fed. He was a great friend; I awaited him anxiously and he must have felt as I did. The albatrosses frightened him, but they too used to quarrel among themselves until only the biggest and strongest remained in the field.

On the 1st of November I decided to mend the mainsail and reinforce it by sewing in large patches. As I worked on it I thought of the friends who designed and made it and who would have been amused to see me at work. To spread the sail out in the cabin, I had to anchor it at every possible point; and each time I had sewn a foot, these points had to be shifted. In the course of the first thirty stitches the needle slipped off the palm and stuck into my hand; this technique was soon abandoned, for

76

however painfully, I got the hang of it. The work was finished in four hours.

I then made a surprising discovery: there was a fly aboard. Where could it have come from? Was it hatched on board? As a good host I offered it some sugar; it buzzed around and then perched on my hand.

Later on, weather permitting, it used to make short flights outside; sometimes it would light on the sunny side of the sail and then, having taken its constitutional, return to the cabin. It was a well-brought-up fly, not one of those impertinent creatures who, out of all the available resting places, chooses your nose; so I took care of it. It was my traveling companion, a good friend who kept me entertained and thus repaid my trouble. Alas! circumstances were too strong for it: it vanished in the course of a storm.

The barometer kept steady at 775, but on the 1st of November I was becalmed and this lasted until the 3rd.

I had done 3,800 miles; what I still had to do was worrying me, for, as the season grew on, cyclones would be more violent; to pass south of Tasmania I should have to go below 44° S.

The glass fell but brought nothing worse than heavy squalls from the N. and N.E. The heavy clouds scattered in the morning and gathered again in the East, which might have led me to believe that I was nearing the Australian continent; but I was sure enough of my navigation to know that these clouds which appeared to be 200 miles away were in reality much farther. My position was in fact 780 miles E. quarter S. of Cape Leeuwin.

One night I was startled to see a whale dead ahead. Fortunately it swerved slightly to port and swam round astern, probably out of pure curiosity. But as it was a dangerous neighbour I persuaded it to go away by flashing an electric torch.

On the 6th of November I felt poorly and was a little feverish; but this passed off. During the night a wave broke over the foredeck with such a crash that I thought *Lehg II* had struck a reef!

The wind, which up to then had been variable, now set in the North, which allowed me to dash along under full sail for several days.

On the 9th I took advantage of a calm to transfer the 50 litres of water from the breaker to the empty tank. It was almost dark brown; and it was all I had left!

After fifty-six days at sea, I shaved for the first time; not that there was any need to do so—I was rather warmer with the beard and would not have minded keeping it. But shaving was something to do for a change.

I thought that the weather was about to improve; but it was wishful thinking and I was disappointed.

The Pilot Chart does not mention fog in this region; nevertheless I became fog-bound for three days. There was, of course, little or no wind; the situation was drastically changed.

"This is the life!" said I to myself. For something to pass the time, I took to reading the accounts of other lone sailors.

I was astonished at the amount of trouble they had with sails and top-hamper; it was doubtless due to the slowness of their crossings. Perhaps they used machine-sewn sails, made of unsuitable material or badly set. I was always careful to leave plenty of grease; the canvas is thus much less susceptible to changes in the weather. On the other hand, my boat was well balanced, and answered very sweetly to the helm; more than ever, I am convinced that two masts is the ideal rig for ocean sailing. This is confirmed by the fact that I had been using the same set of sails since leaving Buenos Aires and that it was to bring me home again. The only changes were to take in the storm trysail or to replace it by the big Bermuda mainsail when weather permitted.

I had forgotten the taste of sterilized milk long ago; on the 10th of November I discovered a bottle whilst inspecting the hold. What a treat!

The barometer fell sharply and I spent an uneasy night; and as daylight crept through the portholes I rose slowly and drearily to get some underwear on my poor old carcass—how it still managed to carry on, I don't know, after all it had undergone in the way of wounds, knocks, strain, cold and near-starvation. Underwear? A sack lined with bits of newspaper and that was that. The contact with my body of something cold, which was not the tepid sea-water of the wash-basin, made me jump. But outside the rising storm was calling. What matter what my body felt? The practised fingers could not be more sensitive; they curved like the talons of a bird of prey, they were claws. See them unfastening a knot here, to make another elsewhere! A mast, a scrap of canvas, what protection are they against the malice of the storm? At least I would not have the wind full in my face.

The ground swell looked harmless enough. The sky was overcast and grey as lead. In the West, low black clouds seemed to be massing for the attack. A gust ruffled the back of the sea. For the moment the minutes were passing rather quickly; later on, when the hurricane was unleashed, they would go more slowly. Up yonder, a scrap of dirty cotton-wool pelted into the East, followed by smaller scraps—like a hyena with its young. Already the sea was breaking into sharp, jagged blades that dissolved to white spray. The new waves clashed against those of a past storm and this battle of giants left great patches of spume; finally, nothing remained but a smooth patch of emerald green water. The wind howled in the rigging.

The glass was at 740 and still dropping. It had never been so low; I knew that one hell of a cyclone was coming, that *Lehg II* would be in the middle of it and that I was about to face a decisive battle. Looking into the cabin and thinking of what was brewing, I put up a prayer to little St. Teresa and sat down. A long look at everything around me, at my bits and pieces, silent friends and companions, at my universe. Returning to the cockpit, I tapped the barometer; it fell to 732. On deck, the view was truly impressive; clouds that looked like black smoke formed a backcloth for a tragedy. An enormous wave shook the boat and by the crash I could guess at the damage below. I peered into the cabin. The bookcase, which was well secured, had been flung across the cabin. The bunks were littered with broken bottles and scraps of cordage in unholy disorder. A horrid sight. One thinks of one's skin and then, noting that the heart still beats, one weeps over secondary matters, one bewails broken bottles and objects which a few moments back hardly counted at all.

I had experienced a miracle.

The weather was and continued to be execrable, but the impact had passed. The crucial instant, the moment of life or death, had produced no more serious consequences. I could not complain; I was able to struggle on. At midnight I lowered the storm trysail and went below to enjoy a well-earned rest. One more battle was won.

After this memorable day the barometer rose. My runs, after one of 113 miles, gradually lessened. On the 13th of November I was only 130 miles from the South-west of Australia, little more than the entrance of the English Channel. But only extreme necessity and real urgency would have made me change my course for a landfall. I had resolved since I left the Cape to make New Zealand in one stage.

Now there were more days of calm, with breezes that died away as soon as they arose.

I had practically crossed the Indian Ocean.

SIXTEEN

SLOW DEATH

I HAD TAKEN TO NOTING each day the distance made and how much was still to be covered; it was something to do.

That day, for example, I had only done 40 miles. It was the first of many similar days; evidently I had entered a zone of calms and I did not know how long I would have to stay there.

On the 15th of November, my position was 37°74′ S. by 113° E. When making my calculations I noticed that it was Sunday. When would that word come to mean anything to me again? There was a long way to go: 2,800 miles to the end of this hard, hard stage.

Next day I passed the meridian of Cape Leeuwin. The look of the cloud bank to the North confirmed my calculations. Any mistake in latitude might land me in some very unpleasant surprises and I could run no risks. Having no motor and relying entirely on sail, I should be in danger close to the land if becalmed, as I now was.

That night a cachalot nearly 50 feet long made a couple of passes at *Lehg II*.

I set the mainsail, which I had not used since I patched it twenty-seven days back, and looked upon my work with pride. It was childish but profoundly human. Steering and nautical astronomy are not enough; a sailor must be many men—cook, nurse or doctor; he sews a sail or mends his sock when an insolent great toe has pushed through. I had patched my trousers with a scrap of code flag.

I was beginning to worry over the fresh water question; what I had left was getting dark and muddy and it was dwindling. My gums were painful; and that is the first symptom of scurvy. I knew well how this disease, which in former times would plough terrible gaps in a crew, begins with ulceration of the gums and skin, loosening of the teeth and softening of scar tissue. Common contributory factors are prolonged cold, damp, bad or insufficient food, but especially the lack of fresh vegetables. It usually appears after sixty days at sea; I had done 65. Had I not been careful to dose myself with vitamin C throughout the voyage I might never have made any port at all. And in spite of my precautions the first symptoms had appeared.

On the 18th I was 130 miles South of Albany, a town and port of South Australia. For sixty-five days I had seen neither land nor ships and had spoken to no one; and yet, against every natural inclination, nothing would have induced me to put in there.

I was still a long way from rounding Tasmania, indeed some 1,440 miles. But I remembered the sound Chinese proverb: "The road of a thousand *li* begins with a step."

One day followed another in restful monotony. I took advantage of it to sunbathe. Although it was only 14°C. in the cabin, the sun on deck was warm and I was grateful to it for two blessings: these baths and dry clothes. But the latter were so impregnated with salt that as soon as they were in the shade—that is, when I put them on—they became damp again.

No birds around me, no sign of life. I do not agree with those who interpret this as a sign of bad weather. I believe simply that the lack of wind makes it harder for birds to fly.

I took in the log which had registered only 64 miles in the last eight hours because without any way, it simply dangled and acted as a kind of sea anchor. The breeze was soft, gentle, peaceful; but it meant exasperating delay. Bougainville, sailing slowly and painfully towards the New Hebrides, wrote: "Rations are the same for officers and the lower deck: but the meat is so bad that we prefer such rats as we can catch." Yet he added: "The men did not ask for double pay, and ill-nourished though they were, they danced every night."

Heroic times. A day like today would have brought the word of command: "Hoist the topgallants!"

In those days they used to say: "Wind in the tail, not far to sail," or: "Sea calm, wind in tail, Sancho Panza goes for a sail." Where are the days of look-outs in the crow's-nest of a galley? "A capful of wind is better than a galley's sweeps," shows how powerful is the force of wind on sails, compared to the muscles of the strongest crew.

Another saying proclaims that "each spar carries its own sail;" everyone can carry his own sail without crowding it on others.

Influenced perhaps by these reminiscences of old navies, I set my balloon jib, or spinnaker if you like, for the first time: 645 square feet of light canvas which should catch the least puff of wind. But there was not enough breeze to keep my balloon from deflating gracefully on the foredeck.

SEVENTEEN

"UPON A PAINTED OCEAN"

"I HAVE PRACTICALLY ARRIVED at the antemeridian of my country; that is to say, I still have to sail half-way round the world." I could not affirm that these lines would or would not be read by anyone else. Soon, at any moment, my brave boat and I might go together to our last rest. But I could not find the right words to convey the atmosphere of that time. Peace, eternal peace, of an inconceivable profundity. Today, as yesterday and for several days, banks of glaucous clouds like marble hung motionless in the sky.

Ten days now, of total immobility, of absolute calm, in the course of which I had not heard the faintest sound. I felt unreal. I remembered Bruges la Morte, the city of the painted dead. Strolling there one afternoon I was startled to hear the steps of a *concierge*. A human being! Here, I required an effort of the imagination to conceive that the world of men existed. I was like a musical instrument that had vibrated with melodies of every kind—Beethoven's symphonies, Saint-Saens' *Danse Macabre* and Wagner's convolutions—and was now being lulled by the serenity of an *Ave Maria*. The familiar objects round me seemed dead; *Lehg II* must be dead. Was I losing my mind?

At last a manifestation of life—my Cape pigeon, whom I had not seen for a long time. He flew twice round the boat and disappeared. I had time to appreciate the magnificent white pattern on his dark wings.

Then there were whales. The sun struck down on the metallic mirror of the sea and a faint vapour was rising. The milky clouds mingled with the water so that no horizon was discernible. The stertorous breathing of the whales sounded like a far-off naval bombardment, punctuated by the splash of projectiles.

I lived. I ate, always the same thing. I could only open tins of corned beef; they were much too large and, once opened, they went bad in a couple of days. This meat made me feel thirsty and water was scarce.

The thermometer rose to 22°C. My potatoes had not only sprouted but were producing new ones. With my constant sun-baths, I was getting as black as a Papuan. Numerous small fish played round me; jellyfish a yard wide floated by, trailing long yellow filaments. Whales came quite close and it was interesting to watch their games.

On the 22nd of November at nightfall I crossed the meridian 120° E., the antipodes of my country. From now on I should be getting closer to it.

The star Actenar rose practically dead ahead. Between the shrouds was Aldebaran and abeam, a little above the horizon, Aries. A moonlit night brilliant with stars, calm, calm and still calm. I took in the balloon jib and replaced it by the storm jib, for the sky was getting overcast.

My hope . . . my hope was a storm. It was all very well to be in the zone of "roaring winds," they refused to play. At last, at first light on the 23rd, the storm blew up but, to my surprise from the East.

I was no longer accustomed to waves and their size was like a new experience. What was really strange was that the entire sky turned brown. It was the "williewaws."

The English chart says: "Rather rarely one of these small cyclones visits our Australian coasts, accompanied by heavy rain and thick low clouds, with lightning. This spectacular phenomenon usually heralds a gale. It is announced by a sharp fall of the barometer; if the fall stops at the end of the day, danger is to be expected; navigators should exercise great care."

Well, that was what was happening. I thought of the Rio de la Plata when the *pampero* was blowing up.

There was no doubt; I must receive the williewaws with full honours. In the meantime it was best to get some sleep, for the visitor would certainly not arrive before daybreak.

EIGHTEEN

THE VISITOR ARRIVES

ON THE 24TH AT FOUR in the morning I was awakened by a heavy list. I leapt on deck, for the boat was broadside on the waves.

The wind was violent. I got some leeway on, and saw that the jib sheet had parted at the first gust.

Accustomed as I was to heavy weather in the Indian Ocean, I kept under full sail, for I had decided to take a risk in spite of a wind gusting at a speed of over 50 knots. I felt that I had to settle the "southern Tasmania question" and to make up for lost time at any price.

The gale was very like my familiar *pampero*.

When night fell I did not hesitate to let the boat sail herself under full sail in the South wind; and although some squalls exceeded 50 knots, and the speed was correspondingly high, I went at daybreak to work out on the bowsprit to replace a line that had carried away. Wrapped in my oilskin—two seaman's knives fastened to my arms so that they would come to my hand with a jerk, this operation was not funny. But it had to be done.

The wind was so violent that the flogging of the storm jib shattered the thimble, and another gust broke a new 20 mm. rope off short. I had to keep my eye on two enemies; the flogging jib which could have damaged me severely, and the sea into which I plunged from time to time.

While taking a breather I saw a little whale to port playing under his mother's watchful eye. At last I managed to finish my work and pull myself together in the cabin, where I stuffed some more newspapers under my wet underwear. My body was covered with red patches and my hands were bleeding, but the job was done.

The wind flew from South to West, the sky being still overcast, and dropped after daybreak. The glass rose very high—to 775—and stayed there. The temperature was 14°C.

On the following night large luminous patches appeared on the water, increasing as I progressed eastward. They were very remarkable. I seemed to be sailing over braziers. Some were over 300 yards in diameter. This phosphorescence is produced by enormous numbers of microscopic creatures called globigerina. Some patches looked like cylinders about 2 feet long. Sometimes they switched off and on like lighthouses and might almost have given the impression of being near an inhabited coast. I thought of the Bay of Naples.

On the 28th of November I was only 400 miles from Kangaroo Island, the southern limit of the great bay of Adelaide. I had been seventy-five days at sea and was aiming for the southern coast of Tasmania. My pigeon friend continued his visits.

Great flights of birds southward bound indicated the direction of the land whence they came and of the quarter from which the wind would come.

My progress slowed up once more. Up to the present the region of calms had not quite tallied with the data of the Pilot Chart. The zone where I was now sailing was shown as being subject to eleven to fourteen gales a month and only four days of calm; whereas I had already experienced ten. I should say relative calm, for my runs were from 50 to 80 miles. On the 30th of November I was 600 miles West of Melbourne.

I began to use salt water for cooking in order to economize my fresh water, such as it was.

The South wind was very welcome; it made it possible to run

at 7 knots and to leave the helm and rest. But it was not entirely reliable.

My clothes were in rags, my oilskin covered with patches. But I had to make do with it. As regards food, the position was not too bad.

I was longing to see the coast of Tasmania. At midday I tried to take a sight, for that is the only moment when one can really rely on one's observation. In the middle of this procedure I lost the pencil with which I was noting a series of altitudes; a wave put a full stop to the proceedings by obliging me to take refuge below and search wildly for something to dry sextant, chronometer, and even the log-book.

Days of mist and fresh winds followed. The waves were very different from those which had rocked me up to the present, for the depth was much less, rising gradually from 2,500 to 900 fathoms. It was evident that I was nearing Tasmania, which I could not see for mist, although on the 8th I was less than 50 miles from the coast where Mts. Picton, Adamson, South Cape and others rise up to 3,500 feet.

Low visibility made it imperative to keep a sharp look-out for this coast, which I very much wanted to see in order to confirm the accuracy of my navigation after eighty-five days out of sight of land, and to check my chronometer.

During the night of the 9th the atmosphere at last cleared, and I was able for the first time to observe the Aurora Australis. The rays piercing the night mists flickered fanwise, like searchlights seeking enemy aircraft; had I not been quite certain that only eternal snows and uninhabited lands lay in that direction, I might have believed it to be the reflected lights of a city.

The sun rose in a clear sky. At 06.00, to the N.W., the monotony of so many days was broken by the appearance first of smoke then of a ship steaming at top speed on the same course. I was no longer alone now. Two hours later, a ship steaming south emerged from the morning mists which had not quite cleared. Ahead to the East the conning-tower of a submarine emerged, only to vanish immediately.

A strong current had carried me off my course to the North. I was now only 22 miles W. of South-west Cape; unfortunately, the wind dropped and a heavy mist returned during the morning and hung about for the rest of the day.

I spent a very uneasy night; I was so close to the coast that I might easily have run on the rocks, and I waited anxiously for daylight.

Joy!

On the eastern horizon, between patches of mist, I saw Tasmania!

The South-west wind freshened and allowed me to take bearings, which reassured me that my chronometer was only 1½ minutes fast. Newstone Islands appeared, one after the other, and I left South-west Cape astern.

Land was so near that numerous birds came to inspect me; it looked deserted. Maatsuyken Island seemed to be joined to the mainland by Witt Island. To the West, relatively shallow water (but still 100 fathoms) was causing the sea to break. Ahead lay White Stone, covered with foam (hence the name) and Eddystone, standing some 20 miles off the mainland. Eddystone Rock is remarkable: a cylindrical mass of rock jutting out of the sea.

I did not wish to go far from the coast, for after rounding Tasmania I would run into a current flowing southward along the East coast of Australia, which would carry me well out of my course. I therefore set my course for those rocks; even with mist I would see them soon enough to steer clear, which would not have been so easy on another course. From time to time I tried to spot them with a telescope.

It was barely two in the afternoon when something which at first I took for a sail showed me that they were near. As I drew closer the waves became more dangerous. The green of the sea was a welcome change for eyes accustomed to the blue of great depths. At 16.00 hrs. the rocks were abeam to the North, while the mist gradually devoured the coastline.

The elation I felt at having made a successful landfall was momentary and it was followed by intense depression—a nervous reaction from the long, hard fight. I had not the courage to face the 60 miles that separated me from Hobart, the capital of Tasmania; a town was in front me and I did not react. It was too tempting: another little effort, 1,200 miles, and I would finish my run and be free from the danger of cyclones.

On the morning of the 11th of December the outline of Tasman Point showed through the mist: it divides Entrecasteaux Channel from Storm Bay. At midday, Cape Pillar, an outpost of the island, appeared far to the North. The wind was still in the South and the cold was cruel.

I dozed off in the cockpit; when I awoke, two cachalots, each over 30 feet long, were swimming alongside. As soon as I made a movement they disappeared.

That night, when shortening sail, I tore a muscle in my left leg.

The weather was now bad; the gale did not let up for a minute. It was quite a job to prepare any food. I took advantage of spare moments to rest. The tack of the storm jib carried away, and once again I had to mend it, playing figureheads against a sinister background. The colours of the clouds were strange and squall after squall came over, laden with rain and hail.

On the morning of the 13th there was a slight lull. The barometer had fallen to 763; the porpoises were rushing round in circles at high speed and for some reason this game worried me. The sea, the air and I were shut up in an atmosphere that varied from mauve to black. A cyclone was coming. I had neither will power nor perhaps strength to lower the mainsail, and I left *Lehg II* under full sail.

The glass fell to 760 and the first blast of the hurricane shook the boat so that I expected to see the mast go by the board. I kept anxious watch for any damage to my sail.

Hope slowly sank as the hours passed; this storm would never let me out of its teeth. An enormous wave over 60 feet high, not uncommon in this zone during a cyclone, broke on board, submerged me and flooded the cockpit. I emerged slowly in a mattress of foam; water was running out through all the scuppers. In spite of my weakness and the troublesome injury to my leg, it was absolutely essential to bale.

Early in the night I tried to keep awake but it was impossible. Gradually, as in a vision, fantastic shapes of ruined buildings flickered ahead. At moments I felt myself falling from a scaffolding. The whistling wind went through the heavy cap I was wearing. The load of innumerable days weighed me down and smothered my reactions; sleep was irresistible.

The boat was no longer on her course; the binnacle light seemed to be mocking me as I yawed from one course to another in spite of myself.

At times I tried to pull myself together, with very temporary success; I soon felt as though I were holding up an iron bridge. I resolved to lower the mainsail. Aching and bleeding, I managed it with great difficulty. The rolling and pitching tossed me from one side to the other like a rag doll, and every blow meant a new wound or bruise.

I cannot express the difficulty I had in mastering that canvas, to stow it away on deck; only I can know what I endured and the relief I felt when at last I could go below and let myself sink down, anywhere.

The boat sailed on without lights. Only the sepulchral glow from the binnacle showed any trace of life on that poor bundle of planks, tossed ceaselessly to and fro by the waves.

NINETEEN

NO CAN CHEW

THE NIGHTS WERE SHORT—only five or six hours of darkness.

My mouth was very painful. The first symptoms of scurvy, mitigated by the vitamins I took, were succeeded by an inflammation of the gums which gave me great pain every time I endeavoured to eat hard biscuit.

On the 16th of December my position was 46°39′ S. by 160° E.; less than 160 miles from Cape Providence, the southern point of New Zealand; but my goal was Wellington, on the strait which separates North and South Islands, so I had still 800 miles to sail. The seams of my oilskin had been resewn so often that it was no longer of much use.

A cyclone from the Antarctic reached me; its epicentre, a compact mass of clouds, melted into the surface of the sea. Immense rays like the spokes of some gigantic wheel appeared in a half-circle to the N.N.E. As I was trying to calculate their trajectory in order to avoid them, something delightful materialized out of this inferno; something that I had missed for several days: my Cape pigeon! The faithful bird had not abandoned me.

He settled on the water and I went quickly to get some biscuit. Having fulfilled my side of the contract, I turned my attention to the cyclone, which gave no time to talk to my friend but increased in violence. The waves pursued, caught and pounded *Lehg II*. Next day they were even more gigantic.

But it was a tremendous satisfaction to note that my daily runs exceeded 150 miles and reached a maximum of 175.

94

Yet I was weak and aching and the hull creaked; I needed all the experience acquired in years of navigation to save *Lehg II*. I would luff or present the stern to the most threatening of the roaring waves that flung me at terrific speed into the troughs. This game went on to the point of exhaustion till, early on the 18th of December, the weather changed. The cyclone? I had already forgotten it: 175 miles in twenty-four hours was rich compensation.

I stripped off my now useless clothes and put on an old raincoat; the short rest and a fine day were enough to put me on my feet again. The wind was a mild south-westerly breeze which carried me slowly towards the coast of New Zealand. Already I could see albatrosses playing; I listened to the rustle of the water along the outside of the hull. I hung my "linen" in the sun to dry and took advantage of the fine weather to make and mend.

I was careful not to sail too near the coast, for it would have been difficult to claw off it if another storm arose; indeed, the weather was uncertain and the sky was occasionally overcast.

A seal came to keep me company; he was hunting a fish. The pursuit was fascinating to watch, as hunter and hunted dashed around the boat and under the keel. They were unconcerned by the presence of a spectator and sometimes splashed me as they leapt. Now and then the seal would stop for breath, inhale deeply and start afresh. I watched the game for a quarter of an hour but I cannot say whether the seal won; I only know that he followed in the wake of *Lehg II*, no doubt in the hope of another chance.

My bird had not reappeared and I was not to see him again.

On the 23rd, reckoning my position to be 42° S. by 170°45′ E., I decided to set on a course for land and have a look for the coast. Visibility was very bad; the clouds did not allow me to take good sights—only a meridian. Even so, the sun looked misshapen. The wind, which had been from South to South-west for some days, now climbed over West to North-west and dropped to a light breeze. In the afternoon, I estimated that Cape Foul-wind lay some 40 miles to the N.E.

As time went on the situation was becoming critical, for if I made the smallest error in navigation I was lost for certain: and that would have been too deplorable after having achieved the "impossible."

And that very night the wind went back into the West and blew a gale. No lighthouse in sight; inky darkness and a chorus of groans and creaks.

Imperturbably the boat rode the waves with magnificent courage and toughness; it was really wonderful to see her under way on these stormy nights.

On the 24th of December, Christmas Eve, at 16.00 hrs., through what seamen call the land mist, a precipitous coast appeared about a quarter of a mile away. It was Cape Farewell, the northernmost point of South Island, staring me in the face. After 101 days land ahead. The stupefying fact was that I was only a quarter of a mile out in my reckoning. I could congratulate myself!

I tried to run as far as possible into Cook Strait; as I progressed the coastline that ends at Farewell Spit unfolded itself before me. A tremendous swell helped me on. Around me bits of tim-ber and branches were floating, but the coast was deserted, show-ing no sign of life. As night was about to fall, I decided to lower the mainsail and let her heave-to to the North, so as to get some sleep before carrying on in daylight; a necessary precaution on an unfamiliar coast.

It was cold on Christmas morning and I suffered from the 11°C and especially from my caloric deficiency. Cook Strait is about 65 miles wide. Being at the foot of Mount Egmont, which is 8,260 feet high, I was surprised not to see it. But no matter; I was sure of my navigation.

The day passed by. At four in the afternoon I was absorbed by the battle of Titans going on round Mount Egmont, which had shown itself for a few seconds. The low clouds, striking the foot of the mountain and jostled on by those following, were whirling at such a fantastic speed that, as an airman, I could think of no aircraft to compete with it—the fastest machine would, in comparison, appear to be stalling. The clouds rushed, rolling, boiling and twisting, to the summit of the mountain. I could imagine what a roaring inferno it was up there, and by analogy I caught an inkling of the incandescent stages of the earth's formation. Everything here spoke of primeval times, the more so as no sign of animal life appeared. Drifting along the current was the wreckage of forests, roots and broken branches that tossed and beckoned to the sky as they rolled. The latter was overcast with an indescribable palette of tattered clouds, black, blue and red, casting strange shadows on the sea. Wherever I looked I was aware of the harsh exuberance of cold, hostile nature; of cold that pierced into the marrow of my bones—the dark vindictive cold of inaccessible spaces, without pity or mercy for any creatures. And I, with my unfortunate *Lehg II*, was sailing into this hell. I would not give up. Hope and some tiny inward glow sustained and heartened me. I was firmly convinced that whatever lay before me, sinister though it might be, must be mild in comparison with my sufferings on the ocean I had just crossed.

I leapt below to snatch a piece of chocolate, green with mould. I rubbed it on the sleeve of my oilskin and ate it with great pleasure. I followed my course along the centre of the strait, which closes in to the East, as accurately as though I could see the coast. According to my calculations, I should have to alter course S.E. at 21.00 hours to follow the curve of the land. At 23.00 the flashes from the lighthouse on Stephens Island pierced the darkness, the first artificial light testifying to the existence of other human beings. I had made no mistake in navigation. The wind was in the West and very fresh; I could not relax my vigilance for a single moment and I longed for daylight.

At dawn I spied Kapiti Island through the morning mist. As the sun rose it showed me Gore Point, Queen Charlotte Point and, farther South, the Two Brothers. The high peaks of this island showed in their full beauty. One of them, its summit white with snow, stood out against a sky of purest blue; below the peak God had adorned it with a mantle of lilac velvet that faded into pale green as it neared the sea. A magnificent present to the lonely pilgrim.

Time flew even faster than my keel; and if yesterday I was unconcerned with delay, I was now conscious of an imperious, aching need to have done. I was exhausted, rigid with cold and dreaming of the rest I might perhaps find that very night.

I was quite near Port Nicholson and expected to arrive shortly; but the wind which had been so favourable dropped as I rounded North Point. As if to try me again, *Lehg II* dragged along. At 16.00 hours I was quite near the entrance to the sound; the high walls of that immense corridor were only 10 miles away! With a fair wind, an hour or two would have brought me to the rest I longed for. But what I got was an uncompromising head wind, a fresh breeze from the North. I sailed as close as I could in order to strike the entrance; but, alas! the current was so strong that I lost ground on every tack.

I saw ships coming out and others patrolling quite near me, but would not understand; they did not even recognize my ensign. I attracted their attention, they came near—and off they went again! No doubt they took me for a member of the local Yacht Club out for a spin.

For the sixth time I crossed the entrance channel and for the sixth time I was farther away than before. Finally I got sick of the game. I lowered the mainsail, went below and collapsed.

But not for long. After a few hours I picked myself up. My first instinct was to get something hot inside me; and seeing the uselessness of my efforts to make port today against a head wind, I decided to wait. Perhaps the old saying: "North wind lost, look for it in the South" would fulfil its promise.

During the night I took bearings on the lighthouse to get my position. I could see the reflection of the city lights in the sky.

Early in the morning of the 27th of December the North wind dropped, and after a period of calm it veered to the South. At last I was nearing the coast, admiring lovely houses dotted along the shore. Past Luhrs Rocks, I found myself in Lyall Bay, an enchanting sight, and passed between the reefs and the small lighthouse on East Point. I was running free with a fresh breeze under full sail up the channel. Off Worser, I luffed and went alongside the harbour launch to show my papers. Surprise. . . .

"Where have you come from?"

Should I say "from America," "from South Africa" or "from the Cape?" I hesitated, then decided that the last might sound more familiar to them.

They looked at me strangely, obviously wondering whether I was mad or sane. I expressed myself with difficulty; my lips moved, but it seemed to me that it was not my lips that spoke.

My interrogators seemed surprised and not really convinced. They gave me a cup of tea and asked me innumerable questions while we exchanged cigarettes.

They notified the port and I received permission to proceed; and so I left these friends of a moment with whom I had broken the silence of long months. As I passed Karalck Bay people were bathing on the beach. The houses along the coast seemed to be hung on the steep slope like birdcages; they were like a great mosaic, resplendent in the sun.

From Kam Point a large circular bay opened before me; I tacked to the West and saw right at the end the docks of Wellington. The wind was now almost dead ahead. A few small sailing boats passed me, going towards the opposite shore; it was Sunday and they must have been off on a pleasure trip whilst I was finishing . . . something rather different.

I saw a Customs officer making signs at me from the pierhead and came alongside. Several people helped me to make fast and I took advantage of this to lower my sails immediately; it was not easy, for the canvas was stiff and the halyards were not running well through the blocks. From first to last it was a long hour's work before I could sit down on deck to rest. And just then someone said to me:

"I say, you can't stay there. Set your sails again and get out into that little dock over there, about 10 yards; the quarantine people will come and see you."

I was dumbfounded.

"Oh! Oh no, I'm not budging from here," I replied forcefully. "Do you know what it's like to spend 104 days at sea? You saw that it took me an hour to stow my sails and now you're asking me to do another hour's work? No, and No! I'm *not* moving."

They called a tug to take me to the appointed spot. A doctor questioned me from the quay.

"Are you in good health?"

"Very good."

"No illness?"

"None whatever."

He and his assistant looked at each other.

"Well, what more do you want? You've only got to look at him!"

And that was the inspection.

Once I was in my berth, crowds of people came aboard: Customs officers, police, etc. One George Law told me that he had lived many years in the Argentine; he was a Lieutenant R.N. He spoke a little Spanish, but we understood each other better with my limited English. He asked me to wait a bit and returned half an hour later with a complete meal, including fruit and cold beer.

Everyone kept asking questions: they wanted to know everything that had happened to me, how I managed to cross the immense Indian Ocean. I tried to answer but it tired me; and once confronted with George Law's marvellous feast I lapsed into silence.

I spent the night alone on board; unfortunately the berth was very bad. The ground swell could be felt and the boat was bumping about dangerously. So next day when the Commodore of the Yacht Club and various V.I.P.s arrived I asked to be moved. I felt that I had to leave *Lehg II* in a nice quiet spot before going to stretch my legs ashore; for the sailor must always think first of his ship.

Two hours later I moored in the Boat Harbour among American warships, a privilege which I owe to the kindness of the chief of the U.S. Naval Base.

My boat was now safe and I could think of myself.

I lived through all these little incidents with great intensity; one cannot resume normality all at once. It was not until I went ashore in a lounge suit, and at the precise moment when a young girl asked me for an autograph, that I looked back at my boat riding quietly a few yards away and realized—at last—what had happened.

Behind me lay a great part of the Impossible Route. For the first time in the history of the world a lone man had accomplished the formidable task of sailing 7,400 miles non-stop from South Africa to New Zealand. No less than 104 days of solitude had been endured on the high seas—a perilous solitude, replete with mischance, struggles, despair and faith that somehow survived to carry on in a hell where I will never, *never* sail again.

Never will it leave my memory.

And, giving one last thought to all I had left behind me, tracing the imaginary line of my route through the Tasman Sea and the grim Indian Ocean, I shuddered.

TWENTY

CITY OF THE WINDS

THE CENTRAL PART of Wellington, called by Kipling "The City of the Winds," is built on a narrow strip of ground bordering the bay. It is curious to see how the tramway has to wind and twist in some places to achieve net gain of a few hundred yards. But I prefer not to lose my way in detailed descriptions, firstly because they lie outside the scope of this account, and particularly because it is not possible in a few weeks to penetrate the life of a people which it has taken generations to shape. Respect for other people's work restrains me from expatiating on my own impressions. In this connexion I remember the remark of a certain newspaper correspondent. Arriving in a large city where he was supposed to spend a week, he had to remain two months because of the war. As he was leaving, an official asked him whether he intended writing of what he had seen. He replied: "If I had stayed a week, I should certainly have done so; but as I have been here two months, I can't. I know less about you now than before I started."

Nevertheless, a few stories of my stay in Wellington are worth telling.

Firstly, the tale of the telegram.

I had an enormous correspondence from New Zealand, generously offering me hospitality so that I could have a restful stay and exchange reminiscences of my country, also many telegrams from South America. One of these was very thrilling indeed.

One morning I was walking in the town as I usually did, when a car stopped by me and a girl from the Post Office got out.

"Good morning, Mr. Dumas," said she, "here's a telegram."

I expected one of the usual messages of congratulation. But, having read it, I promptly sat down on the grass verge. A gardener stopped work and asked solicitously:

"Bad news?"

Passers-by were stopping; the girl who brought the telegram looked worried and asked:

"What's happened? Are you all right?"

I read out the telegram to my improvised audience. After congratulations, it went on: "If you need money, ask."

There was a general burst of merriment. And then and there I composed my reply, writing on the wing of the car. Everyone helped to make it as concise as possible; and this is what I wrote:

"Thanks. Stop. Yes. Stop. Immediately."

Do not forget that I landed in Wellington with £2 in my pocket.

I HAD SOME very happy times in this port, sometimes in warships, sometimes in a fine flat where we did our own cooking. The oddest thing about these feasts was that we used no tables; even when ladies were present, we ate sitting on the floor like Arabs.

The days went by. Repairs to *Lehg II*, not at all serious considering the rough passage, were carried out with the kind collaboration of British and U.S. sailors who were for the moment kicking their heels in the port. I paid them with what remained of my whisky: with two bottles I could pass as a millionaire.

I spent New Year's Eve, a time of memories, in the company of some airmen friends. We sang New Year songs; but we were all far from home, voices grew sad and a laugh was not always echoed.

The house of the Meadows family became a real home for me. Their prodigal hospitality was all-embracing. Often they came with me to buy the necessary stores I was beginning to get together. Invariably after dinner we went to the pictures, then returned to the house for tea and conversation before I went back on board. And every night I went down the little staircase, Mrs. Meadows was careful to remind me:

"Don't forget: there are nine steps!"

I had to count these steps in the dark before I got to the garden path bordered with flowers and ferns. The warning was never omitted and never unheeded; I always counted the steps. I came to think of that refuge as "the house of the nine steps."

I used to take long walks with Mr. Meadows during which we talked largely travel. He had been very fond of roaming. He was born in England, had been in Canada and Central America, where he had learnt a fair amount of Spanish; after several voyages, he had settled in Wellington with his Scottish wife and two daughters.

AND SO WE CAME to the 30th of January, the day on which I had resolved to sail.

I slept at the Meadows' house and went down the little flight

of steps for the last time. It was daylight and no warning was uttered; but I counted the steps all the same. The little path with its border of flowers and ferns led me to the dark green gate with its number in white. I closed it behind me and went slowly down Tinakori Street. All the houses there are surrounded by trees and flowers; it was a sunny morning. I turned into Park Street running downhill through the older part of Wellington with its timber houses. After a few blocks I passed the largest wooden building in the world. And with my head in the clouds, hardly thinking of what I had to do, I found myself at the dockside. Mechanically I bought a number of copies of the morning paper, *Dominion*. Reality returned. Some of the pages would serve to refresh my memory, others to protect me against cold and wet, if my experiences in the Indian Ocean were to be renewed.

TWENTY-ONE

THE DASH FOR AMERICA

SOME SAILOR FRIENDS filled my one tank with water; I had not had the broken one repaired, for with the breaker and the demi-john I should have 160 litres. Another friend gave me something precious—a pair of gum boots. I was also given a silver ashtray adorned with a kiwi (the bird of New Zealand), a hamper of fruit and vegetables, a case of beer and half a dozen bottles of lemon juice. A cinema operator recorded the scene as the Meadows family presented me with an album of views of New Zealand and a carved wood kiwi.

The wind was in the North, and as I could not get out under sail, a picket boat with the Spanish name of *Vagabundo* took me in tow. All my friends were aboard. I told the skipper to stop and wait whilst I set sail. I set the mizzen, then the staysail. At that moment, rounding the pierhead, *Lehg II* came into violent con-tact with a concrete pillar. The damage should have been repaired; but no. I had decided to go and go I would; the job could wait till later.

Setting the staysail was not without danger, for the wind had freshened and the sea was getting up. What would it be like out-side? Having set the storm jib, I cast off the tow. Farewells were shouted, and my friends made for harbour as the heavy seas made navigation difficult.

It was 11.00 hours, Saturday the 30th of January 1943. Under her own sail, the boat soon got way in the channel and the now familiar shore-line went by.

The wind was up to 40 knots and was whipping the waves into spray. The ships anchored in the roads dipped their ensigns and I replied.

In Palliser Bay, no longer sheltered by the hills, the wind found its full force and the choppy seas, increased by the ground swell, were making their presence felt. The waves were short and high and broke on deck, drenching everything. One wave carried away a boat-hook. Taken by surprise, I had not even had time to put on my oilskin and was soaked to the skin: I was furious at getting into this state before I had even reached the open sea. At 17.00 with a tremendous swell I passed Cape Palliser, the last outpost of this country that I might never see again.

Physically I was in good shape. During my stay in Wellington all traces of scurvy had vanished.

My eyes left the dimming coast to gaze ahead into the immense Pacific Ocean. It was over 5,000 miles to Chile without any port of call on my course. Only Chatham Islands lay near it, a little to the South but very close to my point of departure. In spite of what lay ahead of me I was very happy; once on the coast of Chile I would be nearly round the world.

The glass remained very low at 758, the temperature at 18° and relative humidity at 80 per cent.

I remained at the helm all night and it was not until the morning of the 31st that, the wind having slackened off a little, I decided to get some sleep.

The weather improved. The wind, having swung to the South, stayed there. It was a gentle breeze; the sky was lighter and the clouds vaporous.

On the 1st of February I crossed the 1800 meridian of Greenwich and was back in West longitude. The barometer fell to 756. Finding myself in the tail of a cyclone travelling N.N.W. to S.S.E., I decided to take in the mainsail. Up to the present my progress had been excellent, but the storm was getting worse and the glass dropped to 752. That night I narrowly escaped disaster, passing very close to the floating trunk of an enormous tree.

Lehg II was making a great deal of water, no doubt through the knock she had sustained on leaving harbour; but in this weather repairs were out of the question.

On the morning of the 2nd the weather eased a little. A shark over 10 feet long was swimming alongside with a pilot fish in attendance. I recognized the characteristic black stripes. The shark swam under the keel and came so close that I could not resist the temptation to shoot him. He was hit in the back and dived at top speed.

I took advantage of the light breeze to throw my bags of spoilt potatoes overboard, keeping only the new potatoes that had grown from them. My harvest! In the afternoon I saw some sharks and whales.

During these first days in the Pacific I had to adapt myself to conditions very different from those in the Indian Ocean. The waves are not nearly so long, the clouds are higher and I rarely noticed any mist. The sun shone frequently. The West wind on which I had counted refused to settle, playing between North and West. I was suspicious of the unknown and kept my eye on the barometer to guard against any unpleasant surprise.

On Friday the 5th I was some 600 miles East of New Zealand. On the 8th I decided to inspect the damage to the hull, hoping that it was only a graze; but I found a plank cracked. I repaired it with a strip of inner tube, stuck on with paint and held in place by a plank which I screwed on. No more water coming in—except for the waves that broke on deck.

The Pacific was tranquil; any mist made the sky appear grey and the sea the colour of lead. As the wind was in the North-west I could often leave the helm.

Hidden alongside a panel in the cabin I discovered one of my jack-knives which I thought was lost. Before going on deck I cut myself a piece of New Zealand bread with it: when I emerged I had the fright of my life. *Lehg II* had run on the rocks. I was paralysed for a moment.

No. The boat was only elbowing her way between two whales. With a puff of wind, she tried to climb up one of the shining backs, then slipped off again. The seconds were interminable. What was the whales' reaction going to be? Perhaps the creature being jostled by my hull thought that his companion was being playful. They seemed to be asleep. There was nothing to be done. *Lehg II* had got herself into a jam and must get herself out of it. I did not dare to move for fear of startling the monsters.

Quietly, purposefully, with exasperating slowness, the boat pushed her way through alone. At last she was clear and left these uncommon obstacles astern. I drew a deep breath and my heart resumed its beat.

My diet was more varied than on the earlier part of the voyage. Apart from the inevitable chocolate with biscuits and butter, I ate apples, peaches and various little luxuries. There were several boxes of sweets, a quantity of dried fruit, nuts, raisins and figs—even some Christmas pudding! A lordly life, in fact. *Lehg II* was making 135 miles a day. At night I saw shooting stars; the wind would blow into the quarter where they fell.

The mist became thick, like clouds of smoke whirling on the sea. This was not serious, though the humidity reached 100 per cent. The current was carrying me towards my far-off goal and there was rarely a day on which I could not see the horizon. I thought of the Indian Ocean, where it was only visible from the wave crests. Here the sea was gentle, truly Pacific, getting more tranquil as I went on. The albatrosses here were brown with black underwings (the fuliginous albatross).

Raratonga, in the Cook Islands, lay 600 miles to the North and Polynesia farther off on my port bow. Perhaps one day when the world found peace again I could go there with some kindred spirits who shared my taste for aimless wandering at sea. I was satisfied enough with my lot to daydream of other voyages; an idea that would certainly not have occurred to me in the Indian Ocean! It was marvellous not to be constantly shipping seas.

Petrels appeared; sharks were abundant and I had time to watch them. I could do anything I pleased; I had banquets — menus such as: tomato soup, salmon, cheese, dessert, with beer. . . . Sometimes the wind showed signs of freshening, but it dropped at nightfall. I would predict the next day's weather by observing the sunset; for example, if the sun set fiery red I would have a day of fresh winds.

The ocean was 90 per cent calm. Only the ground swell athwart my course day and night, telling of far-off gales, made the boat rock lazily. Conditions were unfamiliar and she seemed to feel it too.

At dawn on the 15th I was 240 miles from the Maria Theresa Reef and 1,300 miles South of Tahiti; the nearest island was Rapa, 900 miles to the N.N.E.

Walking carelessly on the deckhouse, I made a false step, fell down the hatch and received a violent blow in the short ribs. It was so severe as to compress the lung on that side and for a short time I felt that I was suffocating. It was extremely painful and, though I soon recovered, I was unable for a long time to stand quite upright.

The unforeseen! . . .

In this splendid weather I left the portholes open to dry out the cabin. I slept, I read and I ate. The chef would dish up *rice a la Kia-Ora*, full of delicious oddments—so named in honour of my New Zealand friends. The only snag was the pain which kept me from moving freely and obliged me to wear a bandage over my ribs.

It was at this moment that the head winds began to blow; rather than beat to windward I hove to. The barometer rose to 7800 and the temperature was 17°C.

Normally I slept all night. I had breakfast in the morning, lunch at midday, and in the evening, rice with cheese or whatever came to hand; many different things go with rice.

In this atmosphere of deep peace many ideas turned over in my mind: planning future routes, choosing friends for a cruise, building, with the knowledge born of long experience, the ideal boat. I imagined that others, too would be impelled to throw over the routine that stifles life and open their minds.

My thoughts ran, they flew: far across the sea from port to port and picture to picture. After a day of hard work in a town, human beings feel the need of "noble leisure," as the Greeks called it; here this leisure possessed me utterly, feeding and thriving on my soul. The inner world is a gift of God and one should make the most of it. But why did my fancy stray so far? Why dream of other horizons and plan travels whilst I travelled? Strange urge, to be gone when one has not yet arrived.

One tranquil day succeeded another. I would tap the barometer and find it still at 784. My mind revolved between this happiness, the accursed pain in my ribs—for it hurt me to breathe—memories, and the thought that I still had so far to go. Then memories grow painful; and seamen mumble them over sourly as they pace the deck. The truly indispensable entertainment is work; and lacking occupation, introspection becomes a danger.

At last a freshening breeze blew me out of it. On the 18th I made 123 miles. From then on I stayed longer at the helm in order to make my runs as long as possible—sometimes as long as sixteen to eighteen hours.

I planned to make the most of the favourable winds of this latitude as far as the 90th meridian and from there work up to Valparaiso in Chile, which lies on 33° S. But the winds seldom obeyed the Pilot Chart and were reluctant to blow from the West; furthermore, mist was 50 per cent more frequent than the Chart laid down.

I had long forgotten what a cyclone was like. The relative calm of the Pacific is certainly due to the immense expanse of sea without land masses; aerial currents flow freely, whereas in the Indian Ocean the tropical heat, being unable to escape to the North, runs along the East coast of Africa. Hence the waterspouts which I experienced. West of Australia the same phenomenon occurs; the winds, interrupted in their normal course by the land mass, follow a trajectory that brings them into conflict with those of the Antarctic, producing the storms that cost me such anxiety and hardship.

This is true to the extent that the sun, setting towards the North, causes heavy mists and calm in the zone where I was now navigating.

To allow *Lehg II* to run more freely, I lightened her forward by moving the anchor chain to the foot of the mainmast.

The leak remained slight; yet I had to bale half a bucket of water every two hours to keep her dry.

The relative comfort of *Lehg II* can be judged by the fact that I had on board some silk underwear and even a dinner jacket, still quite undamaged; if I did not always cook, it was not because of the weather, for the cooker, hung in gimbals, remained horizontal whatever the angle of the boat. Justifiable inertia was the reason.

On the 20th the barometer dropped 15 mm. Elsewhere, that could mean a gale; but here, all that came was a S.W. wind that had no effect on the swell and did not make the seas break. The only point worthy of notice was ground swell from the Antarctic.

My runs varied between 100 and 130 miles: 470 miles in four days.

As the wind veered to the South, I took advantage of it to go down a bit in latitude (towards the Equator), to 42°17′; but there I found quite unreasonably calm weather. I made use of it to touch up the paint on the hull, leaning over the gunwale. I also caulked the waterways on deck: I climbed the mainmast to reinforce the steel halyard tie, which looked unsafe.

The thought of being alone in the immense Pacific was somewhat unsettling.

I did not draw away from the latitude of the "roaring winds;" on the contrary, I sought them, I needed them. But here they roared rather gently. The barometer might fall 15 mm., they did not materialize: at the best, a light, good-tempered little breeze dispersed the clouds or herded them together, played with them and with the back of a slumbering ocean. I hoped that the conjunction of the moon and the sun would bring a change; it brought none. After wandering through the tropics I was beginning to know these vague, formless, transparent nebulosities, swimming in the atmosphere.

It worried me to see the provisions dwindling away without any corresponding progress. And it was precisely in such weather that I ate more. Lots of fuel and few miles to show for it! I rang the changes on the sails, I tried more favourable zones; I was whistling for a wind.

At the end of February I had done 2,400 miles; there were 2,700 still to go.

I was glad to see mendicant petrels again; they were not as lively or as expert in snapping up crumbs as their cousins in the Indian Ocean. Every night, phosphorescent patches such as I had seen off Australia and Tasmania lit wide stretches of sea; it was some compensation.

The log-line hung vertical from the stern.

I chewed over the idea for seventy hours before making up my mind to set the spinnaker. Once I had made the decision and got everything ready, a gentle breeze sprang up—ahead. Not wishing to get on the wrong side of luck, I packed up the whole bag of tricks. At midnight the little breeze obligingly veered; I brought up the spinnaker again and set it at last.

TWENTY-TWO

WHOSE LITTLE SLIPPER?

HAVING SET THE JIB, I looked round and, floating on the water I saw . . . a woman's slipper, pink, with a pompon somewhat darker in shade; it seemed to be silk.

I built up a romance on it. From its appearance it must have belonged to an elegant lady, a little foot, barely size 4. However did she lose it? Headlong flight? Shipwreck? A lovers' tiff? A scene—or a moment of hesitation? Like the assorted litter of a battlefield, this small object had been swept away in the vast ocean. It was strangely touching. . . .

I was still becalmed. Cigarette ends piled up in the sardine tin, my ashtray. Whales came so near that I had to discourage them with shots or with flashes from my electric torch. Their excessive familiarity was too disturbing.

On the 4th of March I saw a westbound ship, but so far away that she could not have seen me. A little wind from the Southeast broke the sheet of the spinnaker and I decided to take it in. Two days later I saw many birds, probably from Pitcairn Island, 900 miles to the North, where some descendants of the *Bounty* mutineers still live. The ship's rudder was salved in 1932.

The glass fell to 760 and this time it seemed to be in earnest. My old friends the squalls arrived with heavy gales from the North. The cross-seas took *Lehg II* by the shoulder and shook her, but, with all sail set, she travelled at top speed. I made 150 miles in twenty-four hours and stayed at the helm for forty hours at a stretch to make the most of the wind. I got very wet and tired, but anything was better than calms that prolonged the journey. When I went below after those long hours on watch I gave *Lehg II* her head, lashing the tiller on one quarter with a running knot to the other to give some elasticity; it was the only way to manage. The exact position had to be determined by trial and error for four or five hours before leaving the helm, for a couple of centimetres either way would have sent my very responsive *Lehg II* off her course. The angle of the tiller was, as a rule, 2 inches to windward of the axis of the boat.

On the 9th of March, being at 40°41′ S. by 117°15′ W., I reckoned that it would take me twenty-eight more sailing days to reach Valparaiso. But, of course, everything depended on the wind. Storms helped me along, fine weather held me back.

Up to the present I had had no occasion to use a storm trysail in the Pacific.

Once the storm had blown over, winds were variable. Squalls, mist, rain and calm succeeded each other as the days went slowly by. My log kept on repeating these words. Sometimes I saw lightning to the North.

To prevent the continued gybing of the mainsail and mizzen when becalmed, I put up false guys.

I had changed none of my tackle since leaving Buenos Aires, but squalls, gales and general strain had produced a normal degree of wear in the sails; I mended them as required. I was delighted with my equipment; maintenance had been very light and I had no complaints. My one regret was to have lost the only screwdriver on board, just as I was constructing a housing for the binnacle out of an empty box; the lamp had a bad habit of going out at crucial moments. It was an old fault; I remembered how it had let me down on that terrible "night of breakers" during my trip from France to the Argentine in 1932.

Birds continued to fly past; an indication of the land where I was bound. A few hours' flight for them meant long days of navigation for me. I hope not to be taken for a liar when I affirm that at such times I looked back with regrets to old days of struggle against a background of awful majesty. Then, the wind drove battalions of thick clouds, charging down without respite; the boat flew and her wake melted into the enormous waves. What a contrast with present "navigation without trace!" Then, the tense emotion of a struggle for life, second by second, upheld by a deep faith in victory, a will to survive the unbridled fury of the storm. My eyes would light on a halyard, my mind would calculate its breaking strain. And now—this languid progress, so different from the conception of the Infernal Route that the boat herself seemed bored with it. She was built to withstand harsh seas; navigation for young ladies was not her cup of tea. I was with her heart and soul, and I used to pour out my indignation on the pages of the log; and when a storm threatened I retired to the cabin. I had heard that one before.

TWENTY-THREE

THE LAST SLICE

ON SUNDAY THE 28TH I entered the last time-belt of my circumnavigation, having passed 90° W.

I was in the cabin when I heard a noise on deck and found that the main halyards had parted. It was the work of a few moments to set the storm trysail with a flying halyard. I then took a sight and found that I had covered 330 of the 360° of the earth. All I needed now was a little jump of 15° to get home; but when I reached Valparaiso I would still have to do 3,000 miles—round Cape Horn at that—in order to cover the 700 miles, as the crow flies, that separated me from Buenos Aires.

The fall of the mainsail was an omen. A gale from the East soon turned into a raging storm. The wind was over 50 knots and I had to take in the storm trysail in order to tack to the South; by the morning of Monday the 29th, with so little sail, I made 187 miles to the South. The barometer stayed at 760. I spent most of the time lying in the cabin; it was pointless to remain on deck.

Next day the wind was very fresh, due East; my route to the South was making me drift westward; so I decided to go about and set a course to the North. The boat shuddered and creaked; we took knock upon knock, and as I badly needed something hot the stove had to go on strike. So I spent thirty hours without a chance of drinking anything really warming. Feeling thoroughly exasperated, I then had to settle down to changing the nipples of the stove; it took me four hours; but the cup of chocolate I made seemed so delicious that I could not recall ever having tasted anything better.

On April 1st the gale was so kind as to give me enough time to set the storm trysail. I resumed my course to the North-east whilst I mended the mainsail. I was 400 miles West of Mocha Island and had left latitude 40. The sea remained choppy and visibility bad; I was surrounded by mist and great masses of cloud. I had now entered the Humboldt current and felt its favourable influence.

By the 6th of April I was at 36°7′ S. On this latitude, yonder in the East, lay Las Flores, a little village in the province of Buenos Aires which I know very well. I was doing 70 to 90 miles a day.

I was nearing the South American mainland after all; that was the bright side of the picture. After a bad storm some compensation usually emerges.

A mass of warm air was trying to displace the prevailing cold; I was right in the neutral zone and found myself becalmed. Luckily on the evening of the 8th the boat showed signs of answering better to the helm; I was entering a zone of wind.

An enormous cachalot cutting across my bows nearly caused a catastrophe; just as I was about to hit him, he dived with astounding speed. Nothing worse than a fright; I waved him my thanks.

I was thrilled at the thought of approaching my goal and looked forward eagerly to the moment when Point Curaumillas would show through the mists.

The next day a stiff breeze picked me up and I thought that I might very soon be there; but the 10th dawned deplorably calm. The sky, which had cleared after the bad weather, was blotted out by ever-thickening mists—so thick that a number of coastal birds seemed to have got lost. Some of them looked exhausted

and alighted for a rest on *Lehg II*. I had to welcome these unexpected guests and, as a good host, to give them lunch.

What surprised me most was the total absence of shipping,
only 43 miles from the coast.

On Sunday the 11th of April at 20.00 after seventy-one days
out of sight of land I came on deck to see the lights of Point
Curaumillas flashing ahead, a few points to starboard. There lay
Valparaiso; once more my navigation had been faultless.

Next day I could see the coast, but, with the light breeze, my
pace slowed down as my impatience increased. At 10.00 I saw
two fishing vessels to the North, but to my regret they got no
nearer. Farther off, ships coming from the North gave me a wide
berth.

I was fascinated by the intense life of the sea; it was swarm-
ing with a variety of creatures. Shortly after midday, thanks to
the South wind, I managed to round the lighthouse point;
at that moment a sailing yacht making for the port under
power appeared in the offing. I made signals but there was no
response.

I was approaching Valparaiso, America, my country; how my
heart bounded! Hills, mountains, houses, woods, a palette of
bright colours spread out before my eyes. At nightfall I was
becalmed off the Punta de los Angeles; and as a diamond lace of
light crept up across the magnificent crescent of Valparaiso Bay,
I could not restrain a cry of admiration. The coast was only 100
metres off, but it was not for me; I could not move. In the silence
of the night I could hear the lighted motor-buses. I could also
hear someone whistling—perhaps a boy. I decided to ask for his
assistance.

"Muchacho," I called.

The whistling stopped for a moment, then started again.

"Do you hear me?"

No reply. The whistling continued.

"Be a good chap and tell the Harbour Master that I'm becalmed; ask if I can get a tow."

At these words the whistling seemed to stop. A short silence. Then it went on again.

Nothing doing; he did not understand that I needed help. I gave up. Nervously, I smoked one cigarette after another and watched the smoke, hoping that it would show the direction of any puff of air. The sails hung, nerveless. *Lehg II* rocked gently; the waves breaking on the shore were getting close. I thought I saw a rock ahead.

But . . . but it was a boat. Someone on board hailed me:

"Was it you adrift this morning?"

"Yes, it was."

"The lighthouse keeper sent us out; here we are. . . ."

They were soon alongside. It was a naval boat manned by petty officers.

They recognized who I was and greeted me warmly. I asked them on board for a drink and gave them the book on the voyage of *Lehg I*. In the meantime, a slight breeze had sprung up and *Lehg II* started drifting away from the boat and the coast. Seeing this, they sent a line and took me in tow whilst I lowered sail. At 22.00 I came alongside the tug *León*; a number of sailors at once came aboard, helped me to make fast and asked me to come ashore. I replied that I was not presentable: in a pilot-coat, oilskin trousers and gum boots, I was even more of a "filibuster" than when I arrived at Cape Town.

"That's all right," they replied. "We're not likely to meet many people tonight."

The dinghy made for the pier and I went ashore with the two P.O.s who were already my friends. I then noticed an officer of the Chilean Navy and hastened to introduce myself.

"Señor, I am Vito Dumas."

He seemed surprised; he looked me up and down and I

observed my companions who were standing to attention. I felt like a prisoner under escort. Finally, I explained that my last landfall had been in New Zealand, and the officer seemed to understand. He congratulated me, not evincing any great conviction that I was telling the truth. I then asked him to excuse me.

He was certainly puzzled.

We went through several narrow streets and called at a number of those little "ports" full of bottles that are found on all coasts of the world. I tried sopaipilla, I tried wine, and at three in the morning began to notice that it was high tide; and in view of the danger of flooding I asked my friends to take me back on board. They felt a little frustrated at missing the last two ports on that cruise. . . .

Back on the deck of *Lehg II*, I thought in my artless way that it was bedtime—at last. My friends rowed off in their boat, but a voice on board the *León* said:

"Hello! you'll have a cup of coffee before you go to bed, won't you?"

Why argue? They must be right.

I went aboard the *León*. To the light of a single candle that made shadows flicker round the little cabin, we started off again, stirring up memories: names of ports, dates, figures. Then they talked about whaling. The hours revolved, the sky was turning grey. We then decided that I should only sleep for an hour, after which they would bring me a saucepan and I would make them some chocolate *a la mode de Lehg II*.

I closed my eyes, exhausted, and to the gentle rocking of the boat, slept like a log.

TWENTY-FOUR

A SECRET IS REVEALED

AT THE BEGINNING of this book I said that I was fully aware of the vicissitudes I should have to undergo in order to acquit myself with credit in an enterprise which I had christened The Impossible Route. I knew that the difficulties would be enormous; they were, in fact, worse than I expected. Yet I had studied the scheme for ten years. Having weighed these risks, I faced them; and any failure could not have been imputed to lack of foresight on my part. My enthusiasm was unconcealed. The hull had been very strongly reinforced; the sails were made of the best materials and their cut and workmanship left nothing to be desired. The rigging enabled me to face the worst weather with entire confidence. Distance travelled, seasons' average runs, all confirmed my calculations. I never trusted to luck; everything was thought out beforehand. And yet, when I arrived at Valparaiso, my joy was not complete. A shadow lay across the road back to Buenos Aires: Cape Horn. Out of the basketful of advice and opinions of this question, very little indeed coincided with my scheme, which I kept to myself. I proposed to disclose it if successful; and I can now do so.

According to the Argentine Nautical Instructions, the best season for navigation in Cape Horn waters was the time when the sun was lowest in the North, that is, between the beginning of June and the 15th of July; midwinter in the Southern Hemisphere. Winds were on an average less violent and one could hope that the passage would not be too bad. In the stillness of my home, duly impressed by horrific prognoses, I checked and re-checked the information available. And each time I felt more inclined to discount the prophets of woe and to stick to my convictions.

And so, having arrived at Valparaiso on the 11th of April, I resolved not to set sail before the end of May. Time enough for a good rest. I did not doubt the excellent intentions of those who gave me contrary advice, but I had confidence in my own plan and I intended to carry it out. A Captain in the Chilean Navy was also of my way of thinking; he believed that the season and the route I had chosen were the most favourable, especially if I could manage to be near the Cape at the full moon.

My repose was relative, for I had to attend a number of receptions. It is always a great joy to me to arrive in port; I like to be taken round by friends; I feel happy and, after so many struggles, human problems take on a new aspect. I am interested in what others are doing, in the thread of lives entirely conditioned by an unchanging environment. Their questions are normal; they are endeavouring to assimilate someone else's experience. On my side, the effort to understand their problems made me forget my own.

My health was good. Soaked practically all the time during the first two stages, I had not had a single cold. I attribute this perfect state of general health to frugal living and the sobriety imposed by circumstances. Excess is the cause of most human troubles. As the doctors say, more people die of overeating than from underfeeding.

And so, from one reception to another, time went by; a time of most pleasant memories. I shall never forget the welcome of the Chilean Naval College, where I had the honour of addressing four hundred cadets and the entire staff. The Commandant presented me with a miniature mast, flying the Chilean flag, with an inscription commemorating my voyage at the foot. Numerous societies made me an honorary member.

Thanks to Admiral Kulchewsky *Lehg II* was hauled up on a slip at the Arsenal for the first time in the voyage and had a thorough overhaul. Worn ropes were replaced; the navigation workshops repaired my chronometer and I was given the set of charts I needed for my journey. From Buenos Aires, I received an oilskin, thigh boots—for mine were in a sorry state—and a tell-tale, the reversed compass by which the course can be checked without leaving the cabin. I spent a very happy night at Concon Beach with the Betteley family, eating local dishes of sea food. Finally, it would be impossible to enumerate all the parties given in my honour.

TWENTY-FIVE

DEAD MAN'S ROAD

EARLY ON SUNDAY MORNING, the 25th of May, I went to Mass; then I fetched my luggage from the hotel. It had been the first time in all my voyage that I had left my "rabbit-hutch" for a bed.

The city was still asleep and the sun was not yet over the mountains when I arrived aboard *Lehg II*.

I was moored astern of the corvette *General Baquedano*, the training ship of the Chilean Navy, where I had often been a guest. With the help of my friends of the Yacht Club, I stowed my stores: wine, spirits, biscuits, quantities of tinned fish; a change from times when I had not been overburdened with such luxuries. I had stores for more than six months and 3,000 miles to sail. It was the shortest leg of the voyage, but also the most tricky. Cook, Bougainville, and all seamen who have navigated in those waters testify to the fact in their books. Hansen, the only lone sailor who had succeeded in rounding Cape Horn from East to West, lay in the depths off the coast of Ancud; only the wreckage of his boat had been found on the rocks. Bernicot and Slocum had chosen to go through the Strait of Magellan.

I knew that a strong current from the West strikes the coast between 37° and 50° S.; it then divides into two branches, one running North, the other South. The danger is the possibility of being surprised by a westerly gale for a couple of days; if the navigator has not had the prudence to steer well clear, he will inevitably be thrown on to the coast. For this reason, my plan

127

was to follow the route of the clippers and eschew the temptation to stop at Valdivia, where the Yacht Club had invited me to
call.

Many friends had come to witness my last preparations, most
of them convinced that they would never see me again; and I
kept stopping work to say goodbye. By 10 o'clock everything was
ready; the mizzen, mainsail, staysail and jib were set. Saying
goodbye for the last time on board the training ship, I noticed a
plaque with the inscription:

> "I have sailed the seas, carrying in my wake the prayers of
> Chilean mothers and in my sails the breath of the firm,
> indomitable spirit of our country."

The breeze was light. My friend Weddod, accompanied by
many assorted persons with whom I had spent pleasant hours,
took me in tow. We passed along the line of ships at anchor,
including a giant Canadian five-master. She had been lying there
for a long time, a sort of black phantom and warning of what
might happen to me in the far South. She carried a cargo of
wood and had tried to round Cape Horn, but storms had bat-
tered her hull to such an extent that leaks had reached danger-
point. Her skipper, seeing that she was near sinking, decided to
give up and return to Valparaiso with all hands pumping desperately. Was something like that waiting for me? The anxious
faces of my friends, whose forced smiles failed to be convincing
in spite of their wish to be encouraging, their hints that it might
be better to give up the attempt, were certainly not good omens
for my departure.

I knew that the problem would be solved for me in the first
mile; as soon as I was thrown on my own resources. To escape
from outside influences, and firmly to implement my decision,
was the only way to defeat "the impossible."

We were soon past the breakwater. I looked back at the

training corvette, where the signal *"Bon voyage"* must have been flying for me; at that distance it was somewhat difficult to see.

At 16.00 hours I cast off the tow in a very light westerly breeze. I made a board to the N.N.W. to give Point Curaumillas a wide berth. The glass stood at 770, the temperature at 15°C., the humidity 88 per cent. During the evening the wind backed a little to the S.W., the coast and its beautiful colours were bathed in sunshine. One more port was behind me in a sailor's life; but this time I was headed for the imponderables of Cape Horn. What of tomorrow? The day died slowly and the sun sank in a cloudless sky. Astern, above the coastal range stood the peak of Aconcagua.

After sunset I went below; alone in my boat after more than a month—I could not help kissing a panel in a surge of affection for my "shipmate."

For the moment I was still a stranger to her; I was so imbued with memory of happy days in Valparaiso, the land of eternal spring, that it seemed to have been a dream. With its curious and diverse buildings, its narrow streets that wind fantastically as they climb, its romantic old houses of the colonial period, the city has something of all times and a little of every country. Valparaiso is unique.

On Monday the 31st the coast was still visible to the East, but hardly distinguishable between the clouds and the banks of morning mist. The current, stronger than the light breeze, had carried me off towards the North, although my course was set westward. About 5 miles to leeward a schooner from Juan Fernandez was heading for Valparaiso.

Although in my position 71°30′ W., I should have been well clear of anything. I thought I heard breakers; I was practically becalmed—it would be. . . . No. The noise came from an enormous school of porpoises approaching ahead.

On the 1st of June the sea was flat, without a wrinkle, with

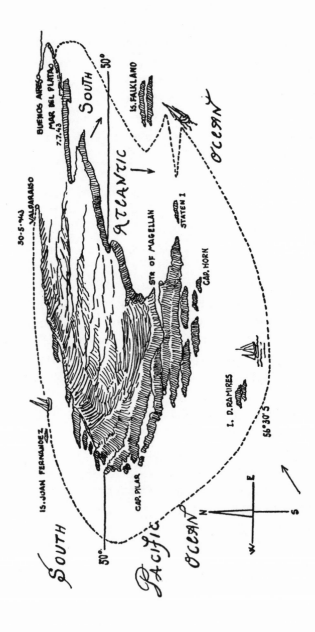

Map showing route taken by *Lehg II* from Valparaiso to Mar Del Plata, via Cape Horn.

little patches of ruffled surface that hardly moved. The wind veered to North-west without freshening much; but by nightfall I was moving well and the boat left a wake of phosphorescence.

On the 2nd of June I caught a better, fresher breeze which allowed me to get some sleep; but the next day it backed to the South, then a little to the South-west. It was intensely humid. I had already travelled 240 miles! Still heading West, and rather wet, I saw ahead Juan Fernandez, "Robinson Crusoe's" island. I came fairly close, but visibility was very bad and I could not distinguish any details whatever.

I noticed a slight leak aft but was unable to track it down. It was barely a trickle; but if it was running in easy weather, it could be a nuisance when I came to a difficult bit. So I made a painstaking search for the crack; but in vain.

On the 4th of June, my position being 34°58′ S by 77°15′ W., I began to drift to the S.W. again, which enabled me to get farther from land and reach the high latitudes.

On the 5th the wind was fairly fresh from the S.S.E.; I could not get out of sight of clouds banked up in successive layers off the coast, which they could not surmount because of the height of the continent. They form a barrier that can stretch over 400 miles from the coast.

I was in the zone of variable squalls with low visibility and other obstacles to accurate taking of sights. The number of albatrosses increased as I went down to the South-west.

Up to then I had been at the helm very little; I spent almost all my time resting in the cabin. The boat was behaving very well, both on and off the wind; the prevailing winds made it necessary to sail close-hauled.

The passage of Cape Horn was gradually taking shape. The whistling of the wind was that typical of these latitudes.

The thick mist left me in semi-darkness. None of these things made any difference to my state of mind, for I was always on the lookout for some new development. Had I begun my voyage around the world by way of Cape Horn, what I found there might have made a deep impression and caused me to worry continually; but, arriving here after such vicissitudes and so much suffering, the only effect was to make me expect the worst. Such weather as this could be compared with my best days in the Indian Ocean. The only difference was the choppiness of the seas, due to the inconsiderable depth.

On the 9th of June the wind seemed to be rising into storm. As I had rested for several days, I took the helm; the barometer had fallen 10 mm. In the daytime I headed into the waves, but at night, with visibility nil and my cow of a binnacle lamp that still persisted in going out, I would not carry on with this form of sport. The boat having lost way, a wave broke over her and me. The shock was so violent and was such a surprise that I felt I was suffocating. We were well under; it was all I could do to hold my breath; asphyxia was near. For interminable seconds I clung to the mizzen mast, or I should have been washed overboard. Slowly, desperately slowly, *Lehg II* emerged: so did I. I took a deep breath. That accursed binnacle lamp and its tricks! I was so furious that, for the first time, I lowered the mainsail and went below to sleep.

On the 10th I set the mainsail again. As I was sailing very close to the wind, the seas were constantly over the deck and it was impossible to do anything without getting completely soaked. It was only in the cockpit, behind a canvas screen that I had had installed in Chile, that I found some degree of comfort, if I may call it that.

In spite of the wind and the sea, *Lehg II* went on unshaken and that was what mattered. She was going towards her goal, but towards the cold, too. Soon it was 5°C. It was no longer much use to stay at the helm, for my hands could not endure the open air for long. Matters came to the point when, having taken in the mainsail to set the storm trysail, I had to burn matches when I went below to warm my numbed fingers. It was ten seconds before I could feel the heat of the flame.

Very close-hauled, the boat was labouring heavily, shaking, shuddering and creaking under the impact of the heavy seas. My position was 42° S. by 82°45′ W.; the wind, which in the last twenty-four hours had swung to the South, obliged me to get a little closer to the land, whereas I had been more than 400 miles off. On the 14th I was level with the Gulf of Penas; I had to bale every three hours, for I had been unable to discover the leak.

Hail came rattling down and the clouds were low. The situation was getting worse every moment. That day I reached latitude 47°. I still had another 10° to make to the South in order to round Cape Horn. Waves were crashing down on board. At night I stayed in the cabin, for it was really disagreeable to remain on deck. Not at all like trade wind sailing in the tropics, when a rainstorm is welcome. Here, wet clothes were piling up in the cabin, which was beginning to look like a slop-shop. Hanging them on a wire was useless; they would not dry. Days were short; the sun barely rose above the horizon.

I was disheartened by the recurring squall and the endless swell; but suddenly I felt that it was vital to go on deck and look round. Why? I don't know. It is one of those odd things that happen to seafaring men. A presentiment inexplicable, as far as our knowledge goes. However that may be, I went on deck . . . and saw an American warship, southward bound and pitching heavily. There were two of us shipping these dirty seas; but we could not make any signals. So we went on our course, each with a different mission.

As the margin of security I had allowed was reduced by the persistence of southerly winds, and I was beginning to get too near the coast, I made a board to the West and, in order not to go too far, took in the storm trysail. On the 16th I was at 48°2′ S. by 82°30′ W. and the wind changing to the South-west, I could resume my course to the South.

The tell-tale which I had installed in the cabin, apart from the very serious deviation caused by the proximity of masses of iron, was useless, as the gimbals had broken and I was not in a position to repair it.

After six days of gales there came a lull and I set the storm trysail once more.

I was 600 miles from Cape Horn. It was time to consider the situations that might arise when I got into the really redoubtable zone. I assessed all the aspects of the problem and drew the most logical conclusion for each of them. This study gave me a more assured plan of navigation.

The cold was so intense that I could not leave the smallest part of my face exposed; on top of the cold, wind and hail lashed down pitilessly. My daily average was 120 miles.

On the night of the 18th of June, Cape Pillar, the entrance to the Strait of Magellan, was 180 miles to the East. This passage tempted me not at all. I had decided to round Cape Horn and neither storms nor risks should shake my determination.

Although not at the helm, I was standing by to surface. Not a detail had escaped me. I had greased two gloves so that the water could not make them useless; I had done the same for my oilskin. I had prepared iron rations on a basis of chocolate, preserves and biscuit for use in the event of being surprised by a spot of weather which might keep me at the helm for several days when close to Diego Ramirez Island, some 30 miles South of the Cape. As it shows no light, constant vigilance is necessary. To keep myself awake, I had benzedrine sulphate ready. Nothing was left to chance, everything had been studied, foreseen and calculated.

I had kept a watchful eye on standing and running rigging in case of wear; they seemed capable of withstanding any unforeseen strain.

As my thigh boots were wet through, I looked about for some means of drying them; and thought of putting a light inside each.

It worked.

TWENTY-SIX

IN SEARCH OF THE ATLANTIC

I WAS BEING CARRIED towards the coast, in the zone of icebergs and drift ice. Numerous birds were flying about, hunting for their living. In the cabin, hermetically sealed, the temperature was 5°C.

On the 20th Cape Horn was 400 miles away to the E.S.E. Getting nearer, getting nearer!

Two days later a storm from the North obliged me to take in the storm trysail for the night. I was already sailing due East; the wind was 40 knots; *Lehg II* went on under mizzen, staysail and storm jib. I was not far from the "mousetrap" and felt that I had to stay at the helm. At 17.00 hours I saw Tierra del Fuego to the North-east and frankly, if the seas were no heavier with the high wind that was now blowing, I could sleep in peace; I had expected worse. Perhaps my imagination had run away with me; if what I had anticipated in the Indian Ocean had been surpassed, I might have exaggerated the difficulties here. I could not deny that the wind was strong, that the waves broke; but *Lehg II* was quite equal to it and was never in danger.

What I had had to suffer to get so far! Out of respect for those gallant sailors of old Spain, for all those who have perished in those desolate regions, I had to admit that the danger existed. Still, I had the impression that I should find calm ahead; and that was what happened. I had come here expecting the worst, though convinced that no difficulty would be insurmountable; expecting the "impossible," I came to believe that I was seeking death; maybe what was really beyond the limit did not appear so to me and I was being irreverent. The memory of the Indian Ocean must have made me feel blasé about all I experienced and it took the sting out of every difficulty.

Towards the end of the afternoon I ran out of the zone of wind into a calmer one, with a clearer sky. To the South I could see, shimmering whitely, the coruscating reflection of the Antarctic ice.

The current was carrying me on my road towards the East. About midday on the 24th the wind veered to the North. Numbers of cormorants came close to inspect the boat; there is nowadays so little navigation in this area that the presence of any ship is a surprise for them. I had still 90 miles to go before striking the longitude of Cape Horn.

That night the north wind had already risen to gale force. I only put my nose outside from time to time to see whether there was anything ahead.

How full of meaning and menace is the sound of those two words: Cape Horn! What a vast and terrible cemetery of seamen lies under this eternally boiling sea! Fear adds its chill to that of the atmosphere, the terror that lurks in a name and the sight of these seas.

Here, everything seems to be attracted and drawn towards the depths, as by some monstrous, supernatural magnet. Had I had a larger surface of wood under my feet, I could have calmed my nerves by pacing the deck, but no; I could not walk my thoughts under control.

Fear of the storm? No. Apprehension that sprang, I felt, from legend, for all that I had been told about these regions. Of all storms, that which lurks invisible in an atmosphere of terror is the worst.

As my boat neared the headland I tried to pierce the unknown with the sword of reason, as though this were my last opportunity to think and to live. Perhaps in a few moments all would be over.

Yet that dim light of my compass on this dark Antarctic night made me look with tenderness on these wrought planks, flesh of the beautiful trees of my country, fashioned by human knowledge into a boat. It seemed to me that they were more in their place on land, living under the murmur of warm light breezes; if they had souls, they would reject the present to which I was exposing them. My voyage had been like a stairway which I ascended step by step, until I found myself here. Here, hard by Cape Horn. Had it been announced to me as a child, I should not have believed it.

They were ringing in my ears with a note of doom, as if they came from the depths of the sea or the height of Heaven, those true words that I could not or would not understand, spoken at Valparaiso before I set out for Cape Horn.

"Wouldn't you like to leave your log here? So that your pains may not be wasted?"

The voice that spoke was trying to be persuasive without sounding ominous. What they wanted to insinuate was quite clear to me: they were not at all confident of my success; they felt that I was lost before I started. But I was full of curiosity about Cape Horn. I wanted to see it, live it, touch it, feel it. . . .

Here in my travelling library, close to me, were the records of Cook, of Bougainville, of so many other navigators, books that I had read and re-read. I remembered the enthusiasm I felt on hearing the news that Al Hansen had succeeded in rounding Cape Horn from East to West, a feat nowise diminished by his terrible end. Hansen had been powerless to escape the curse that broods between the 50° of the Atlantic and the 50° of the Pacific. I felt his Calvary in my flesh only to think of it.

Yet I had taken it upon myself to round the Cape as the only way to make port, refusing to admit any other course. All or nothing. As *Lehg II* neared the grim promontory, through hours made infinitely long by impatience and anxiety, I threw my last card on the table of life.

If luck was against me, it would be easy to say:

"It was lunacy to attempt Cape Horn alone, in a 9-tonner—barely that."

But what if I succeeded?

Imperceptibly, perhaps, the longing of all those who would have liked to make the attempt and were unable to do so, or the hopes of those who had tried without success, crept towards me. Perhaps I had the help of those who perished in this trial; perhaps I was not quite so alone as I thought. Perhaps the seamen of all latitudes were spectators of this struggle against the squalls and the darkness. Perhaps too, this darkness would grow darker yet, that the flickering lantern would cease to glow in front of my eyes, whose lids would close to see nothing any more on earth, now, or ever. This light, of little practical use, was more of an inseparable and invisible companion, standing between me and chaos. Life shone in it, the light of illusion or hope in the possibility—perhaps—of triumph.

IT WAS MIDNIGHT. According to my speed, Cape Horn should now be abeam. The wind was high and the seas heavy. In the cabin I had to cling to hand holds to avoid being thrown against the panels.

Sitting under the light of my little paraffin lamp, I was trying to repair the tell-tale when a shock threw me forward; my face crashed near the deadlight on the other side. The pain was terrible. I was half stunned, but noticed that I was bleeding violently from the nose. Fumbling, I found some cotton-wool and held it to my face to check the bleeding. Then I let myself fall, sick and dizzy, into a corner. It took me several minutes to pull myself together. I did not know exactly what had happened. I feared that the frontal bone might be fractured, in that case, what should I do? Groggy as I was, I succeeded in grasping the situation; I remembered that the boat was still going on and thought of what could happen. I began to explore my jawbone tenderly, looking for a possible fracture. I stopped for a moment. My fingers were wet with blood. No, the chin was all right. The pain was still acute, but my mind was becoming more lucid. As I touched my nose I felt a sharp stab of pain and noticed that there was an abnormal amount of play. So I had a broken nose. Ouf! that was nothing. I decided to look for the worst, for what I most feared: the eyes. I felt them; no damage. What a relief! I continued along the supra-orbital ridge; my fingers found the lips of a wound on the forehead.

After half an hour, a long half-hour, the bleeding began to ease off.

Cape Horn had made me pay toll. Given the speed at which the boat was travelling, I should now be just past it.

For the rest of the night the wind blew furiously from the North; but in the morning it eased off and backed to S.W.

I could not observe the slightest scrap of land; only a bank of clouds to the North indicated its presence. I took advantage of the relative calm to bale; and I made a trip to the mirror to see what it had to say. My face was a horrid mess, swollen, distorted and bloodstained. But that was nothing. I was back in the Atlantic.

TWENTY-SEVEN

DONE IT!

THE 25TH WENT BY, quietly forging on under mizzen, storm trysail, staysail and jib. I remembered that I had left something behind. Oh yes! . . . Cape Horn.

How many sailors have been saddled for life with the consequences of sailing in those parts? As for me, what did I feel? How shall I express the emotion of the first man to round Cape Horn and survive?

A dead sailor was standing by me.

What a joy it was, that sunny morning in 1934, when he came to see me, signed his name on a panel of *Lehg II*, then building, and expressed his approval. He talked of the mother he had left far away in his Norwegian fjord and discussed his plans. It seemed unthinkable that he, with all his determination and optimism, should have finished as he did.

What a loss . . . that he should not have lived to tell, with more talent than I possess, what he felt on rounding Cape Horn. I realized that I was privileged. But . . . what was this privilege worth, even after those fantastic crossings—4,200, 7,400, 5,400 miles—when 1,000 miles still lay between me and my mother? Long, cruelly long were those miles. But, looking back and thinking of the sailors who got no farther, I wept with joy.

ON, ON I HAD TO GO, against a head wind, tacking in a zig-zag that made many miles of very few.

The cold was acute; wind and squalls made it worse, although

141

in this zone the warm currents from the Pacific prevented the water from freezing. I could not stay at the helm for long. Sailing so near the wind, the deck was always awash. Even to catch the sun to make a point was quite a business, for at midday it was only 9° above the horizon and very hard to see. On the 26th, however, I managed to get my position as 45°56′ S. by 61°30′ W., getting clear of the zone of 21 per cent of force 8 gales into another where the percentage was only 17. As I was only some 90 miles East of Staten Island, I decided at nightfall to make a board towards land, so as to avoid the choppy seas by the Barwood Bank.

The wounds in my mouth were a nuisance; they bled every time I tried to eat.

On the evening of the 27th I saw a seal, an indication that land was not far; so, having sailed in low visibility under an overcast sky, I preferred to go on the opposite tack in order to keep away from Staten Island; the approaches there are so dangerous and the seas so heavy that one should give them 20 miles berth. And next morning I found that I was on the bank that I had been trying to avoid; it was violently choppy and beginning to snow. It was annoying not to be able to take a sight, for I did not know how far I was from the Falkland Islands which stretch some distance to the South and include Beauchêne Island and Mintay Reef. I did not want to leave the Falklands to westward, for that would necessitate making a wide circle and take me into a current that would carry me towards the middle of the Atlantic. I could manage the wind and the sea perfectly well; the problem was to locate my position.

It was a year since I had left my country and I had just crossed the 60th meridian. What a lot of things had happened in a year! Every day meant more miles behind, fewer ahead.

It so happened the wind backed to the West late in the afternoon. I spent an uneasy night, fearing an unpleasant surprise.

According to my calculations I was 30 miles from Mintay Reef. I could not see a thing: every time I went on deck the snow lashing my face drove me below again. So the only thing to do was to stay there. The wind was blowing between 30 and 40 knots with a tendency to westing, which helped me on northward. I hoped it would stay there, so that I could give the Falklands a clear berth.

Rarely have I awaited the dawn of a new day with such suspense as I did on the 29th, for in the darkness I could not see where I was sailing and feared that I was rushing on to unforeseen dangers. It was impossible to take a sight. With daylight, my anxiety decreased; but a loud crack brought me up on deck. The backstay shackle had parted under the violent wind which accompanied the rain squalls. Making the most of the rare lulls in the gale, I managed to make it fast; as I was about to go below again, I looked around and, through the squalls, saw the Beaver Islands. What a relief! I was past the Falklands. To the North of these lie the Jason Islands; but if the wind did not change, I should be past them by midnight.

On the 30th of June I was able to take a sight which showed me at 49°55′ S. by 62°30′ W.

Looking ahead now, it was only a question of days; upon my word, I already felt at home. The look of the water, the porpoises, the enormous number of birds flying round *Lehg II*, told me that I was home. No more changes. My course was set for the River Plate now. I had been a month at sea.

The shallow and uneven bottom made short seas which did not trouble me. The mean depth is only 80 fathoms, getting shallower towards the North. The sea that can get up on these thin layers of water is so slight that neither the boat nor I would suffer much, even in the event of a storm.

I had passed Santa Cruz and the coast was some 200 miles to the East. Cape Horn was far away and with it that reasoned pessimism which compelled every other moment to work out plans for all possible contingencies. At that time, I looked forward to the black patch, Dead Man's Road, to resolve my doubts and also to taste the divine satisfaction of not having been mistaken. All that was now past. Even the hardships seemed to have shrunk, viewed at this distance as if through the wrong end of a telescope.

Thanks to sailing close-hauled, everything below was soaked with sea water. The temperature remained at 5°C., but the average runs were excellent. On the 5th of July I was 150 miles from Mar del Plata. The sun, already higher, infused the atmosphere with a friendly warmth that seemed to invite a siesta; the route was gay with birds and beautiful white-sided porpoises. With a fair wind from the West, *Lehg II* was cracking ahead, sailing without interference from me most of the time.

On the morning of the 5th of July I saw a Chilean steamer with a four-master in tow, coming from Buenos Aires. They had a cargo of coal and were bound for the Strait of Magellan. The next day at sunrise was fair; clouds and squalls were behind me.

TWENTY-EIGHT

FOUR MINUTES SLOW

I WAS PLEASANTLY OCCUPIED in making myself a cup of chocolate when, without any particular reason, I looked ahead . . . and there was the coast, less than 5 miles away.

What had happened?

The chronometer was four minutes slow, giving me a difference of 60 miles in longitude. It was Quenquen ahead of me. I was quite indignant, although this discrepancy was understandable; the chronometer had undergone great hardships, shaken up by many days' close sailing, and in particular the oil had congealed. My most immediate reaction was: pack up the sextant and chronometer and from now on sail by sight of land. My fury spared the compass, however . . . I forgot my chocolate and sat down at the helm for a spell of peaceful yachting, with a cigar.

Interminable beaches, yellow dunes, a little tree here and a ranch there; behind them the low hills; shallow, nile-green water. I was having fun with this type of navigation, the only kind that I had never practised in the whole of my journey. As the night fell there was the Mala Cara buoy—an "Ugly Mug" that did not look too bad to me. The moon was in her first quarter; the wind, a gentle breeze off the land. Mar del Plata was only 18 miles away and I came in sight of it in the first minutes of the 7th of July.

The port was there—but the wind dropped. It had favoured me so far: now it was light and dead ahead. I was to the East of Punto Mogotes lighthouse; a little farther to the North the red and white lights of the breakwater marked the finishing post of my trip. Slowly I passed along Fisherman's Bank, giving *Lehg II* a gentle pat; she had been through such a lot. God must have loved her; and thanks be to Him, the end of a terrible Odyssey was very near. How beautiful were the stars! Those in the sky and those on land were twinkling, peaceful and friendly. The air was clear and the flashes from the lighthouse met no obstacle. I could hear the waves breaking on the beach; it was the only sound.

Out of thirty-eight days I had only spent seven at the helm; *Lehg II* had flown home on her own. I could imagine the surprise of people ashore when the ghost came home next day.

And it dawned. The fishing boats sailed by, peopling the bright morning, taking no notice. Finally one of them heard me hailing:

"Ahoy, *amigo*! When you get back from fishing, tell the harbour Master that I'm becalmed. If I could have a tow. . . ."

"We're not going in till the afternoon."

"Never mind! Any time will do."

Off they went. And I was the one to be surprised. They had no idea who they were talking to. So I settled down to cook a lunch which I had been hoping to eat at home. But soon I heard the popping of a motor; the boat passed near me; now she was turning. The fishermen hailed me in their dialect:

"Cap'n! We were waiting for you! We watched out all day hoping to see you come in. We didn't mean to leave you just like that without saying anything."

I swelled with pride. They called me "Captain." They wanted to give me a tow.

"But you'll lose a day's fishing."

"Bah! We fish everyday; the honour of towing you happens once in a lifetime."

I asked them aboard. One of them helped me to furl the sails. We cracked a bottle in honour of the event. They passed a tow. I made it fast to the bitts, and *Lehg II* proceeded sedately towards the harbour. We sang sea shanties. And soon we were in port and looking for a mooring off the Yacht Club. Every face that appeared was bright with excitement. Once safely moored I set out for the Club; as I set foot on land my legs nearly let me down; they were wobbling feebly. Hands and congratulations reached out to me. As I sat on a bench of the Club House, one drew off my boots, another went to run a hot bath for me—how good it was for my chilled body!—a glass of whisky was handed to me. Now two naval officers appeared; one of them wanting to take me to the cabin prepared for me on the Coastal Patrol ship *Belgrano*; his name—believe it or not—was Amour! Everything I expected was beyond my expectations. I was staggering, stammering; all I could say was:

"I hope you're not putting yourselves out."

"Of course not! You'll have everything you need and you'll be among sailors."

My cup was running over. I let myself be towed along, proud as a peacock.

TWENTY-NINE

RECESSIONAL

I COULD NOT HAVE IMAGINED my way of life; I had to experience
it. From the Port Admiral to the last matelot, everyone fussed
over me. Telegrams poured in. Receptions at the Rotary Club,
at the Sailing Club, in private houses. Photographs, press inter-
views, autographs—I was the centre of the world.

On the 9th of July I was bidden to the ceremony of hoisting
the flag at sunrise. The crews of all ships were on parade, silent
and motionless in the dawn. As the rim of the sun climbed into
the pale sky, a bugle call tore the silence and the flag broke from
the mast. I was not alone. The great fraternity of the sea was at
my side.

I offered that moment to God and murmured to myself, to
that particle of the divine that each of us carries within:

"For this—I would go round the world a hundred times."

THIRTY

A LETTER

LEHG II WAS MOORED near the Coastal Patrol vessel; in spite of present delights I had to sail on. I had still 200 miles to go and I could not miss Montevideo. All through the voyage my Uruguayan friends had sustained me with their encouragement. In a letter which I received at Valparaiso, one of them said to me:

"We cannot follow you to share your struggles, but our thoughts are with you, intensely and sincerely; do understand that your triumph will be not only yours but ours as well; do please heave your anchor here."

The value of friendship is something that I have always understood. Wherever friends may be, one must go to them if possible.

That is why, when I set sail one afternoon, it was for a very short run. A huge crowd was assembled on the jetty; warships returning from an exercise saluted, fishermen going out to sea hailed me with good wishes. Only the wind was sulking; but one of the *Belgrano*'s boats towed me from the jetty.

Outside, the wind was from the North and I had to luff; the sea was so calm that the boats convoying me could, and did, fill me up with mates which they passed over the side.

In order not to go too far from the coast I decided to make boards of two hours. Thus I spent a night, a day and the next night. After sailing for over thirty hours with the tiller lashed, I was level with Mar Chiquita. At 22.00 hours I made a board landward. I had only been able to sleep for an hour and a half in all.

149

It was perhaps 22.30 when I scrambled on deck; whether it was the current or just bad luck, but the fact remains that less than 100 yards ahead waves were breaking on the shore. The wind was practically nil. I leapt to the helm to cut it loose, but I had no knife on me. Seconds were passing. Through the mist which exaggerated its size, a high dune suddenly appeared before me; it was rushing at me. I finally succeeded in unlashing the helm and put it hard over: the boat did not respond. The breakers were very close. I tried to luff, but *Lehg II* kept straight on. She lifted on a wave and when she dropped again, I felt a heavy jolt; the keel was on the sands. The following wave broke on deck, breaking the mizzen-stay.

I was desperate; I was suffering with the boat. I kept on repeating: "I am a bad sailor . . . a bad sailor, a bad shipmate; it's my fault. . . ." At the same time I knew that this was not the moment for lamentation; I had to save *Lehg II* by getting her as far up the beach as possible. Holding the tiller and taking advantage of each breaker, I gained inch by inch. Soon the ketch was well aground in the sand; the tiller beating to and fro with every wave.

I must lighten her. It was midnight. Drenched by the waves, I reached the beach some 15 yards away and deposited the dunnage, which I carried over my head to keep it dry. Then I began again.

By the evening of that unhappy day my task was finished and *Lehg II* considerably lighter. I had left the sails set, so that every time she eased, she would get farther inshore; she was now high and dry at low tide. From time to time I went to see how she was getting on, thinking that she would probably never sail again. Every boat that had gone ashore on these beaches had been destroyed.

THIRTY-ONE

THE RESCUE

ON SUNDAY AFTERNOON, somewhat encouraged by the result of my efforts, I decided to go in search of help. From the top of a dune I tried to attract attention by signalling with my arms.

When I was about to give up in despair and return to my camp, a horseman rode up. I gave him a letter for his employer, Señor Arbelay, asking him to inform my friends of my lamentable plight. The man assured me that the message would reach them by Monday morning. I did not conceal the difficulties that would attend any attempt to salve *Lehg II*.

They decided on the simplest course: to pass a tow which would have to be at least a thousand metres long.

The sequel is quite a story.

On Monday afternoon the trawler *Py* and the patrol boat *Mocovi* arrived at the beach where we were stranded. They sent a ship's boat in through the breakers. Lieutenant Antonini studied the position and, as it was getting late, he assured me that he would return next morning with everything needful.

He kept his promise. The trawler, anchored about a kilometre off the coast, passed the cable which I called the "sea serpent" because it did not sink; seeing that the boat could not possibly have brought it in; the cable had been married with another of coir fibre.

It took a whole day to pay it out and make fast to *Lehg II*. When everything was ready the order was given to the trawler: "a kick ahead and stop." Thus *Lehg II* was launched square on to the breakers; very gently without a scratch she was hauled off the beach and refloated. It was a real masterpiece of seamanship. Everyone was pleased; I was even more delighted.

As for myself, I was to rejoin ship by road, with my cargo, in order not to hinder the salvage. Heartfelt thanks to the Ministry of Marine!

THIRTY-TWO

THE YACHT FOR THE JOB

THAT NIGHT SEÑOR ARBELAY took me back to Mar del Plata, following the lorry which the municipality had so kindly lent me to carry my bits and pieces. I could not conceal my apprehension for the boat. Would she have sprung a leak? More wretched worry and delay to round off a voyage which was really finished, for Mar del Plata could reasonably pass as the end of my journey, after sailing across three oceans and rounding Cape Horn. Never mind, I would sleep on the beach; for over a year, I had spent only two months of relative repose on land. If the boat had to go up on the slips for repairs, would the backlash of fatigue not overcome me? What an effort, to start again. . . .

The car purred on. We had little to say to each other. Both of us would have liked to talk, to think of something else; but worry was inexorable.

We stopped for petrol; and there I heard the news. I was astounded; *Lehg II* had not made a drop of water. We started off again full of hope. Step on the gas! Now perhaps I could do something about it and be off again in a day or two. Begone, misery; roll on the happy ending!

So there we were. One afternoon, with a fresh, fair breeze from the South, I sat at the helm of my faithful companion once more.

Let's talk about her.

Her length—31 ft. 2 in., for a deep-sea yacht—is open to criticism. I admit that it may not be ideal.

153

When a journalist asked me my plans, I replied that, if *Lehg II* was bought for a museum, I was thinking of having a 50 ft. boat built. He replied:

"You'll be much happier with a boat like this than with a larger one."

True enough. I was only toying with the illusion of greater convenience; but experience has proved that this length, coupled with a Norwegian stern, gives an excellent hydrostatic performance in any sea, the agility of an acrobat, and especially a flow of water along the hull without leaving eddies. There is very little drag.

The mainmast should not exceed 30 feet above the deck; the only result of making it longer would be to increase the heel in difficult weather. I had noticed that replacing the mainsail by a storm trysail with a surface of a few square metres only had no influence on my daily run. This is so true that when I set the balloon jib one day in a wind of 10 knots to see what would happen, I found that the boat got blanketed in the trough of the waves and behaved less well. The puffs only reached her on the wave crests and she showed a tendency to luff in the troughs, which gave her an abnormal heel. Instead of keeping a steady course, she yawed a great deal.

The two advantages of the Bermuda rig, which are so great that I will have nothing else on any future boat, are: the ease of taking in or setting sail even in a 25 knot wind, and the absence of spars and top-hamper required by a gaff rig; not to mention chafing against the rigging and damage due to sun and salt water. One day a block will jam, another day the lacing if not the peak thimble itself. It may be questioned that for sailing, as I did, mostly before the wind, Marconi rig is right; yet in practice it has always given me the best results.

I had no trouble with the canvas I selected—No. 8, hand-sewn—apart from some rusting of the steel luff clips; I had been unable to procure galvanized ones at the time. This is an extraordinary record for a voyage of this kind.

In 1931 I had tried the experiment of a boat with very tall masts, demonstrating to the yachting world the possibility of taking the high seas with a boat intended for racing like my 8 metre *U.I.* in which I crossed from France to the Argentine. It was the first and the last time.

In the following years naval architects showed a tendency to fine down cruising yachts, giving them relatively high masts. But for such a voyage as I had accomplished, a boat of this type would have been disastrous. Waves sometimes exceeding 60 feet and winds up to 70 knots amply confirmed my belief that a Norwegian, with continuous framing from end to end, has the cohesion necessary to withstand constant terrific shocks. For in my navigation it was no question of a storm here and there, but of an endless succession of dirty weather.

As regards a sea anchor, I have one point of view which settled the question for me: I would never give such an object ship-room. I am convinced that a boat can stand up to any sea, comfortably enough, under sail. She has freedom of movement and can lift to the seas. Should the wind force exceed 50 knots I would say, contrary to the opinion that following combers can play havoc by breaking on deck, that one of my favourite pleasures was to run through squalls on a mattress of foam. My speed on these surf-riding occasions exceeded 15 knots; I then presented the stern to another wave and began this exciting pastime anew. When a wave arrives roaring from astern and it seems impossible that the ship could lift, it stands to reason that one is frightened; but when one has ascertained that fright is not justified, one gets accustomed to the exercise. In these circumstances many people would lay-to; I at once rejected this solution, feeling, as if in my own flesh, the suffering of the boat buried under raging waves. Whatever the hurricane, it never compelled me to strike all sail; my mainsail has no reef points. The old saying which prescribed a salute to squalls by taking in sail was never adhered to in the course of my voyages; when I did take it in it was in order to get some rest.

Nor do I believe in interior ballast, which is dangerous. However carefully it is battened down, it *can* come adrift and the consequences will be disastrous. I have an example of the effect which that kind of projectile can produce in the cabin of a ship. The woodwork below carried visible scars inflicted by the handle of the capstan. I was lucky to have dodged it myself.

As for taking sights, the most frequent difficulty was the motion of the boat. Another major obstacle is the absence of a horizon, masked as it is by the infinity of planes constituted by the waves. If I tried to "shoot the sun" standing up and leaning on the mizzen mast, the water which got into the telescope wetted and blurred the mirror and obliged me to give it up— not to speak of the danger of violent jolts which on several occasions nearly sent me overboard. The best post I have found for observation was seated on the cabin hatchway with only half my body protruding. Thus I could get the sextant under cover quickly if a wave threatened to wet it. In any case, the

operation was always rather like breaking in a colt. I put the chronometer below, in full view, so that I could read it at any moment.

Several times I took circum-meridians, but I must admit that I was rarely able to note with certainty the hour when the sun reached its zenith; generally I made an approximate calculation, averaged from a series. The altitude presented another insoluble problem; the sun, practically always veiled, only allowed observation of the meridian.

I calculated longitude by a very simple method; weather permitting, by the rise and setting of the sun, sometimes in conjunction with those of the moon and a third observation at the moment of taking a sight. The correctness of my calculations was confirmed by the accuracy of landfalls in regions where visibility was very bad.

THIRTY-THREE

WE'RE HERE

A SIREN SHRIEKED.

An oil tanker came up, flying the signal: "Congratulations and best wishes." Passengers and crew applauded me as they passed and asked whether I needed anything. I didn't.

The ship was coming from the South coast and following the same route as myself; but she soon left me behind and by night was no more than a light ahead, soon to be duplicated by another—Querandi lighthouse.

At 21.00 hours I passed the site of my accident. Then Medanos Light appeared. If I continued at this rate I should be at Montevideo in a matter of twenty hours. All this time I could not sleep. One can do that sort of thing once. . . .

Very early in the morning I passed Cape San Antonio. But, alas! as the day wore on the wind dropped. I was steering by compass, but at night the lights of Montevideo were my guide. I did not feel tired. I was wide awake with anticipation, joy . . . and prudence. I ate pleasant food and I drank good wine. And quietly, serenely, full of hope, *Lehg II* surged on through the calm seas, to find herself off Montevideo in the morning. It was a bit slow in this calm and, caressed by the rising sun, I began to doze off in the cockpit.

I was roused by the whistle of a tug, full of friends coming to meet me. I fell on their necks, they on mine. Fatigue fled and we chatted and joked until we arrived at Flores Island, where I had been asked to wait until the next day, Saturday, to make my official entry into the port of Buceo.

158

What a beautiful evening I had with the charming people who live on the island at the foot of the lighthouse! And what a good rest.

On Saturday, at 17.00 hours, in splendid sunlight, very different from the squalls of a farewell which I thought might be the last, I returned.

Cheers, shouts, dinghies, boats, people crowded on the pier, tambourines—the triumphal reception of my arrival in 1943 was repeated. The only difference in the scene was the new building of the Uruguayan Yacht Club.

It would take another book to describe the triumphal progresses and the kindness that were my lot at Montevideo. When I remember these things in my retirement, I am happy to have added one little stone to a fraternity that nothing can ever destroy.

As I was expected at Buenos Aires on Sunday at 11 o'clock, *Lehg II* made the passage under tow lest the wind should fall. And on Sunday the 7th at 10 o'clock, to the deafening sounds of sirens and whistles, of cheers and shouts, I came into my home port and moored on the stroke of 11. On the deck of a Swedish ship moored close by, the Captain and an officer standing under their flag began to lower it slowly. A sudden hush fell. Extraordinary that such a simple act should silence assembled thousands.

As I came on shore the accolade of my friend Commodore Aguirre, the salutes of the officers and finally the embrace of my mother showed how this immense crowd was moved by one feeling and one wish: to celebrate my success; for I had circumnavigated the globe by the Impossible Route.

I AM ENJOYING the evening in a remote place in the Sierra de Cordoba. A dog has dug himself a form to sleep in and I can hear birds twittering. It is only a very gentle whisper; colours merge into darkness, contours fade; night is creeping on the mountains. Down in the valley, lights come alive, blinking like falling stars, each one of them a boat on land that carries its own problems. Silence is falling with the dusk.

I am filled with such happiness that a silent prayer arises from the depths of my being.

"Lord, be lavish of Thy Peace and guide to all the ports of all the world those sailors who are orphaned in the immensity of the sea."

Lehg II sailing near Buceo Harbour at the end of the voyage.

An enthusiastic crowd waiting for Vito Dumas to go ashore at Buenos Aires harbour at the end of his voyage round the world.

PRINCIPAL PASSAGES
OF VITO DUMAS

FIRST VOYAGE

Route No. 1. *Lehg I*

Arcachon—Buenos Aires

6,270 miles = 76 days

Arcachon: D.[†] 13.12.31

Vigo: A.[††] 22.12.31
  (9 days = 550 miles)

Vigo: D. 26.12.31

Las Palmas: A. 11.1.32
  (16 days = 80 miles)

Las Palmas: D. 27.1.32

Rio Grande: A. 13.3.42
  (45 days = 4,200 miles)

Rio Grande: D. 5.4.32

Montevideo: A. 9.4.32
  (4 days = 400 miles)

Montevideo: D. 11.4.32

Buenos Aires: A. 13.4.32
  (2 days = 140 miles)

SECOND VOYAGE

Route No. 2 *Lehg II*

Round the world (7 ports of call)

20,420 miles = 272 days

Buenos Aires: D. 27.6.42

Montevideo: A. 28.6.42
  (1 day = 110 miles)

Montevideo: D. 1.7.42

Cape Town: A. 25.8.42
  (55 days = 4,200 miles)

Cape Town: D. 14.9.42

Wellington: A. 27.12.42
  (104 days = 7,400 miles)

The distances on this table correspond to the actual distance travelled, according to the wind and not to a direct line between ports. Thus, for example, the distance between Buenos Aires and Montevideo is variously drawn, as 110, 140 and 160 sea miles.

[†]D. = Departure
[††]A. = Arrival

Wellington: D. 30.1.43
Valparaiso: A. 12.4.43
  (72 days = 5,200 miles)
Valparaiso: D. 30.5.43
Mar del Plata: A. 7.7.43
  (37 days = 3,200 miles)

Mar del Plata: D. 28.8.43
Montevideo: A. 30.8.43
  (2 days = 200 miles)
Montevideo: D. 6.9.43
Buenos Aires: A. 7.9.43
  (1 day = 110 miles)

THIRD VOYAGE

Route No. 3. *Lehg II*
Buenos Aires—New York—
Azores Islands—Canary Islands
—Buenos Aires
17,045 miles = 235 days
Buenos Aires: D. 1.9.45
Montevideo: A. 3.9.45
  (2 days = 110 miles)
Montevideo: D. 15.9.45
P. del Este: A. 16.9.45
  (1 day = 75 miles)
P. del Este: D. 22.9.45
Rio de Janeiro: A. 19.10.45
  (27 days = 1,300 miles)

Rio de Janeiro: D. 5.1.46
Havana: A. 9.3.46
  (61 days = 5,400 miles)
Havana: D. 2.6.46
New York
Azores Is.
Canary Is.
Cape Verde Is.
Ceará (Brazil): A. 16.9.46
  (106 days = 7,000 miles)
Ceará: D. 5.11.46
Montevideo: A. 10.12.36
  (35 days = 3,000 miles)
Montevideo: D. 26.1.47
Buenos Aires: A. 28.1.47
  (1 day = 110 miles)

FOURTH VOYAGE

Route No. 4. *Sirio*
Buenos Aires—New York
  (one landfall)
7,100 miles = 117 days

Buenos Aires: D. 23.4.55
Bermuda: A. 6.8.55
  (105 days = 6,400 miles)
Bermuda: D. 2.9.55
New York: A. 23.9.55
  (12 days = 1,300 miles)

COMMENTARY ON THE CONCEPTION AND DESIGN OF LEHG II BY MANUEL M. CAMPOS, NAVAL ARCHITECT

THIS BOAT, which I designed in 1933 and built in 1934, was conceived for ocean voyages. Discussion with Vito Dumas led me to choose the Norwegian type as being ideal for sailing before the wind in bad weather, chiefly because of the form of the stern.

This type, which is actually as old as navigation, appears on all seas in innumerable versions. It is so common in Scandinavian countries as to be the national type of sailing vessel.

In the Argentine, before the construction of the port of Buenos Aires, the anchorage off that city was dangerous in almost all winds; hence the use of boats with double stems known as whale-boats which were probably of Spanish or Italian, certainly of Mediterranean origin.

The length of these whale-boats varied from 29 ft. 6 in. to 45 ft. or even 50 ft., but never less than 29 ft. They were peculiarly well adapted for use in this open anchorage. But the tradition had been almost forgotten when, in 1927 or 1928, people in yachting circles began to appreciate the excellent qualities of the Norwegian type. Soon after, several boats were built, copied almost exactly from Atkin's design; he in his turn had been inspired by the celebrated designer of Norwegian double-enders, Colin Archer.

Soon after, again, I received my first order to design a Norwegian; I then remembered the precise details that I had obtained from an old shipwright, shortly before his death, concerning the Rio de la Plata whale-boats of former times: their dimensions, proportions, etc.

In my efforts to collect information concerning Scandinavian boats of the "Norwegian" type, I found that they were in the main heavily

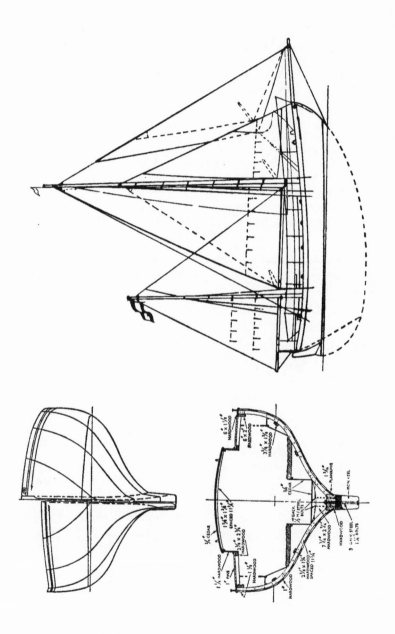

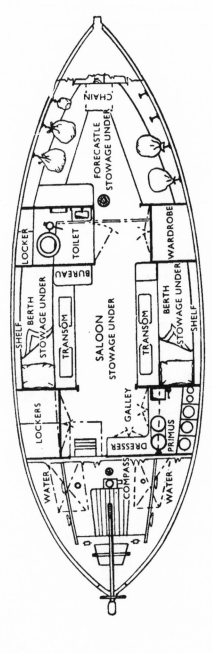

Lehg II. Designed by Manuel M. Campos. Length 31 ft. 2 in.; beam 10 ft. 9 in.; moulded depth 5 ft. 7 in. *Sail area*: mainsail 215 sq. ft.; mizzen 77 sq. ft.; staysail 80 sq. ft.; jib 82 sq. ft.

built fishing boats; naturally enough, since fishing is one of the principal industries of those countries. Others were pilot boats or lifeboats which, for use as yachts, had an excessive displacement and a considerable quantity of interior ballast with its attendant dangers.

Furthermore, their construction was too heavy and their classical gaff rigs looked old-fashioned at a time when Bermuda rig was becoming popular.

Lehg II is a modernized version of the old Rio de la Plata whaleboats, in which the proportion of length to beam has been reduced, after the manner of the classical "Norwegians," and the very considerable ballast (3 tons 9 cwt.) has been converted into a cast-iron keel in order to ensure perfect stability whatever the degree of heel.

The specifications were: keel, ribs, floor timbers and deadwood in general, reinforced and benefiting from the excellent quality of Argentine woods; simplifications of the whole structure of the deck and deck-house. By this means a light and very strong structure can be achieved; all pieces were dovetailed in the traditional manner.

The rig adopted for *Lehg II* was the Marconi ketch, with moderate hoist and sail area, but quite sufficient for single-handed navigation on the high seas. The working was centralized in the cockpit.

I think I may say that the result was satisfactory. The boat turned out to be fairly fast, stable, with a high reserve of buoyancy, easy to steer in all weathers; her owner and skipper considers her fit for navigation on the high seas anywhere and in any weather.

MANUEL M. CAMPOS

OPINION OF VITO DUMAS
ON LEHG II

TO COMMENT ON the qualities of my boat before going to sea might have seemed rather daring; after having gone round the world with her I have got used to singing her praises.

The duet formed by a careful and experienced naval architect and myself, accustomed to ocean sailing in boats of various types, gave a most harmonious result.

As for myself, I am not in the habit of following other people's methods when it comes to navigation; much comment is founded on errors arising from varying interpretations of a given fact.

In the special case of a voyage round the world on the 40th parallel, the problem was complicated by the fact that no precedent existed; the only data I could gather referred to larger ships, adequately manned; and even so, all that was said of this zone was less than encouraging.

As far as my own voyage was concerned, the chief points of discussion were the characteristic features of the regions traversed and the human factors, while other elements were unfairly passed over in silence.

What could I have done on this desolate route, had I not been able to rely upon a suitable craft?

Sudden disaster is always round the corner at sea; danger lies everywhere in the waves, mast, sails, rigging, deck; the possible causes of failure could be extended indefinitely. The truth is that success is the reward of a harmonious combination of factors contributing to the desired result.

Lehg II shipped no water, although combers broke over her almost daily. The hollow mast out of my old boat had been made in France, in a dockyard on the Gironde, and, in spite of winds which sometimes exceeded 70 knots, in spite of the battering of the waves, it remained standing. As a human being who succeeded in surviving, my feelings during successive assaults of a raging sea were those of fair and sincere appreciation of the professional integrity of the joiners who had made that mast, of those who, in my own country, had built the hull, forged the ironwork, sewn the sails; and, last but not least, of the architect. My very real gratitude was that of a man, who, having tempted fate, felt himself sustained by the co-operation of others.

Lehg II's speed was good; on one occasion I made 170 miles in twenty-four hours under staysails and mizzen only; I was to beat this record a few years later with 240 miles in a day north of Brazil, assisted, it is true, by the current.

Yet the boat did not give one the sensation of speed; her progress was even and often, when in the cabin, I underestimated the storm raging outside. With her length of 31 ft. 2 in. she rode the seas perfectly; and her fittings below exceeded in their convenience every wish and every need. I could stow stores and food adequate for a year at sea.

On the other hand, it should not be forgotten that a sailor must get the feel of his boat, assimilate her characteristics, in order to get the best results.

Lehg II was an ideal floating house of extraordinary strength and endurance. But I must point out that the lines and construction of *Lehg II* should not be compared with other "Norwegians" of similar appearance. I might say, to use the phraseology of prefaces to films or novels, that "any resemblance of persons or situations is accidental."

The proof of this is that the "Norwegians" built at the same period as *Lehg II* carried an external ballast of 1¼ to 1½ tons at most for the same length, whereas she carried 3 tons 9 cwt.; on the other hand, I had done everything possible to minimize weight above the waterline. I carried my fad to the point of giving away bits of my rigging to various friends and clubs during earlier voyages—to one, my cross-trees; to another, the gaff of the sail I used before adopting the Marconi rig: all to increase my stability!

To give an idea of the superb construction of this boat, I will only say that when I reached Wellington after the "impossible run" of 164 days in the Indian Ocean, an official who boarded *Lehg II* could not believe his eyes when he looked round the cabin. After 7,400 miles—and what miles—*Lehg II* looked as though she had just come out of the shipyard.

I will finish this brief description of my boat by saying that, thanks to her robust build and her first-class sailing qualities, she gave me full and complete satisfaction.